LEADING
Strategic
CHANGE

DR. KIRIMI BARINE
PROF. DAVID MINJA
DR. JOHN MUHOHO

LEADING STRATEGIC CHANGE

Copyright © 2015 Kirimi Barine, David Minja & John Muhoho

Published by:

integrity
Publishers inc.

P.O. Box 58411,
Raleigh, NC 27658,
U.S.A.
info@integritypublishers.org

ISBN 13: 978-1-937455-24-8

Publishing Consultants:

PUBLISHING
Institute of Africa

www.publishing-institute.org
info@publishing-institute.org

Contents

PART I

Introduction to Strategic Change

> To survive and succeed, every organization will have to turn itself into a change agent. The most effective way to manage change is to create it.
>
> **--Peter Drucker**
>
> The illiterate of the 21st Century will not be those who cannot read and write, but those who cannot learn, unlearn and relearn.
>
> **--Alvin Toffler**
>
> The only constant is change.
>
> **--Heraclitus of Ephesus, A Greek philosopher**

CHAPTER 1

Why Change

In 2002, Kenya ushered in a new political dispensation after the then National Rainbow Coalition (NARC) won the elections that year defeating the independence party, Kenya African National Union (KANU). The enthusiasm among Kenyans for change was so high that they were rated as the most optimistic people in the world at the time. Fast track three years later, the drive for change had died and the optimism dwindled. What happened in between that changed the drive and motivation for change? Are there lessons organizational leaders can learn from this experience?

Heraclitus of Ephesus, a Greek philosopher, known for his doctrine of change being central to the universe, is credited with this statement; *"There is nothing permanent except change. Nothing is permanent except change. The only constant is change. Change is the only constant. Change alone is unchanging."*

The intensity and scope of change is taking place in all spheres of life, from social, political, climatic to economic environments and is having tremendous impact on organizations as well as individuals.

Most of all the developments that we see now including ICT, television, space exploration, globalization, have occurred over a span of a hundred years – and these developments are likely to be accelerated in the new millennium.

The pace of change in current times is more rapid, more complex, more turbulent and more unpredictable than ever before and has affected the very foundation of human existence. Therefore, the question is not whether what is current will become obsolete, but how soon.

Change has always been a feature of organizational life, though many argue that its frequency and magnitude is greater today than ever before (Burns, 2004). According to Barbara and Fleming (2006), the forces that operate to bring about change in organizations can be thought of as winds, which are many and varied- from small summer breezes that merely disturb a few papers to mighty howling gales which cause devastation to structures and operations causing subsequent reorientation of purpose and rebuilding.

Change throughout the ages is encapsulated in the comments of Jones, Palmer, Osterweil and Whitehead (1996) when they observed that:

> As we approach the 21st century, the pace and scale of the change demanded of organizations and those who work within them are enormous. Global competition and the advent of information age, where knowledge is the key resource, have thrown the world of work into disarray. Just as we had to shed the processes, skills and systems of the agricultural era to meet the demands of the industrial era, so we are now having to shed ways of working honed for the industrial to take advantage of opportunities offered by the information age.

Organizations are attempting to recreate themselves and move from the traditional structure to a dynamic new model where people can contribute their creativity, energy and foresight in return for being nurtured, developed and enthused. Most people asked about organizational life today agree that it is becoming ever more uncertain as the pace of change quickens and the future becomes more unpredictable. Academics and business people alike echo this. For instance, looking ahead to the future, Drucker (1988) maintained that by 2008, organizations would be almost wholly information based and that they would resemble more a symphony orchestra than the command and control, managed structures prevalent in the 1980s and 90s.

Levels of organizational change

Organization Level

Theories of change at the organizational level see change as a product of interaction between organizational subsystems and interactions and changes across their boundary with an external environment. Change analysis and intervention tends to be holistic in nature (Stickland, 1998).

Group Level

Another strand of organization change theory focuses on group and team behaviour. At the group level, the change dynamics are viewed in terms of group values, norms and roles and if effective change is to be achieved, then these group characteristics should be identified and understood prior to attempting planned change. Organizational change is seen in terms of interactions, conflicts and relationships between groups, with particular functional or task groups exhibiting cohesive resistance to change (Stickland, 1998).

Individual Level

The last area of organizational change theory is centered upon individual behaviour. At the individual level, emphasis is given to individual needs and motivations in order to counter resistance to change. The individual perspective argues that individuals are best able to cope with and facilitate change if they are involved and empowered to design and initiate it (Kanter 1984 cited in Stickland 1998, p. 44).

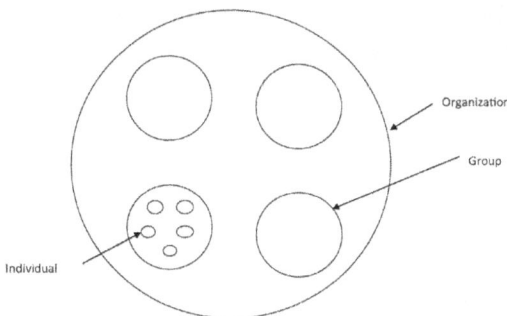

Figure 1: Levels of change

Justification for organization transformation

Globalization of world economies has resulted in high environmental volatility coming in unpredictable ways. As such, environmental changes such as technological and innovation, globalization, regulation and de-regulation and changing consumer behaviour have affected many organizations. Organizations are therefore being challenged to respond to such challenges by reinventing themselves and by enhancing their business processes in order to survive in an environment which has become increasingly competitive (Ansoff, 1987).

In addition, organizations are undertaking strategic changes in order to align their business strategies to the environment thereby matching their resources and activities to that of the environment (Johnson and Scholes, 2002).

In order to cope with the external and internal pressures, organizations must become more innovative, anticipate change and drive it well. The capacity to anticipate change and manage adaptation to it in a timely and acceptable way is one of the key success factors for competitiveness and wealth creation of organizations and economies as a whole. For an organization (or individual for that matter) to survive, it must accept change as a fact of life. It must then proceed to build capacity, skills and competencies and embrace strategies and leadership styles appropriate to match challenges presented by the changing environment (Prosci, 2000).

According to Coch and French (1948), the success of any organization is measured by its success in responding and managing strategic change. Todd (1999) in addition argues that change management must be undertaken in a structured and synthesized approach in order to achieve a sustainable change in human behaviour within an organization.

CHAPTER REVIEW

It is clear that change is inevitable. As Heraclitus puts it, *'The only constant is change'*. In other words, from social, political, climatic to economic environments, the intensity and scope of change is taking place in all spheres of life and is having tremendous impact on organizations as well as individuals.

Today's customer has been noted to be very sensitive and keen to changes in lifestyle, tastes and freshness. Companies should therefore strive to adapt in order to meet the needs of the current customer.

Every organization goes through periods of transformation that can cause stress and uncertainty. To be successful, organizations ought to embrace change. Businesses must develop improved production technologies, create new products desired in the marketplace, implement new administrative systems, and upgrade employees' skills. Organizations that adapt successfully are both profitable and admired.

CHAPTER 2

What is Strategic Change?

S trategic change is defined as a difference in the form, quality, or state over time in an organization's alignment with its external environment (Rajagopalan & Spreitzer, 1997; Van de Ven & Pool, 1995). It can also be defined as the deliberate and coordinated actions taken to transform an organization to achieve its objectives (Johnson and Scholes, 2002).

The business dictionary defines strategic change as the restructuring of an organization's business or marketing plan that is typically performed in order to achieve an important objective. For example, a strategic change might include shifts in a corporation's policies, target market, mission or organizational structure.

According to Hofer and Schendel (1978), strategic change means changing the organizational vision, mission, objectives and the adopted strategy to achieve those objectives. In other words, they define strategic change as "changes in the content of a firm's strategy as defined by its scope, resource deployments, competitive advantages, and synergy."

Change leadership on the other hand, is championing the achievement of intended, real change that meets the enduring vision of an organization. It involves collaboratively developing and implementing ideas to achieve positive change. The change leader learns from other leaders and elders, models the vision, and encourages members of the organization to commit to and champion the vision. The change leader additionally inspires others into new ways of thinking and doing business and routinely energizes the change process and removes barriers to change (Hofer and Schendel, 1978).

According to the United States Government Accountability Office (GAO), change management is defined as:

Activities involved in (1) defining and instilling new values, attitudes, norms, and behaviours within an organization that support new ways of doing work and overcome resistance to change; (2) building consensus among customers and stakeholders on specific changes designed to better meet their needs; and (3) planning, testing, and implementing all aspects of the transition from one organizational structure or business process to another.

Combining definitions from management expert John Kotter and BusinessDictionary.com, is a more succinct take on what it means: Change leadership (1) concerns the driving forces, visions and processes that fuel large scale transformation or (2) is a "style of leadership in which the leader identifies the needed change, creates the vision to guide through inspiration, and executes the change with the commitment of the members of the group."

Types of strategic change

According to the Kaplan Financial Knowledge Bank, change can be classified by the extent of the change required, and the speed with which the change is to be achieved. The four types of strategic change are explained below.

- **Transformation** entails changing an organization's culture. It is a fundamental change that cannot be handled within the existing organizational paradigm.
- **Realignment** does not involve a fundamental reappraisal of the central assumptions and beliefs.

- **Incremental** change can take a long period of time, but results in a fundamentally different organization once completed.
- **Big Bang** change is likely to be a forced, reactive transformation using simultaneous initiatives on many fronts, and often in a relatively short space of time.

	Extent of change	
	Transformation	Realignment
Incremental	**Evolution:** Transformational change implemented gradually through inter-related initiatives; likely to be proactive change undertaken in participation of the need for future change	**Adaptation:** Change undertaken to realign the way in which the organisation operates; implemented in a series of steps
Big Bang	**Revolution:** Transformational change that occurs via simultaneous initiatives on many fronts: • more likely to be forced and reactive because of the changing competitive conditions that the organisation is facing	**Reconstruction:** Change undertaken to realign the way in which the organisation operates with many initiatives implemented simultaneously: • often forced and reactive because of a changing competitive context

Speed of change (left axis label)

Figure 2: Types of Strategic Change

Incremental change is usually the result of a rational analysis and planning process:

☑ There is a desired goal with a specific set of steps for reaching it.

☑ It does not challenge existing assumptions and culture.

☑ It is usually limited in scope and is often reversible.

☑ If the change does not work out, there is a belief that the organization can always return to the old way.

☑ Incremental change usually does not disrupt past patterns - it is an extension of the past.

☑ Management feels that they are in control.

Transformational change involves changing existing structures, the existing organization and the existing culture. It will be a top–down process, initiated and possibly imposed by the top team and may come about because:

- ☑ The organization is faced with major external events that demand such large-scale change.

- ☑ The organization anticipates changes and initiates action to make shifts in its own strategy.

- ☑ Strategic drift leads to deteriorating performance and requires transformational change.

Transformational change differs from incremental change in that it requires new ways of thinking and behaving, is major in scope, discontinuous with the past and is generally irreversible.

Types of organizational change

For many organizations, the last decade has been fraught with restructurings, process enhancements, mergers, acquisitions, and layoffs – all in the hopes of achieving revenue growth, increased profitability and increased customer satisfaction.

According to Chen et al., (2001) the major areas of changes in a company's internal environment include:

- ★ *Strategic:* Sometimes it might be necessary for management to adjust the firm's strategy in order to achieve the goals of the company, or even to change the mission statement of the organization in response to demands of the external environments. Adjusting a company's strategy may involve changing its fundamental approach to doing business that is, the markets it will target, the kinds of products it will sell, how they will be sold, its overall strategic orientation, the level of global activity, and its various partnerships and other joint-business arrangements.

★ *Structural:* Organizations often find it necessary to redesign the structure of the company due to influences from the external environment. Structural changes involve the hierarchy of authority, goals, structural characteristics, administrative procedures, and management systems. Almost all change in how an organization is managed falls under the category of structural change. A structural change may be as simple as implementing a no-smoking policy, or as involved as restructuring the company to meet the customer needs more effectively.

★ *Process-oriented:* Organizations may need to reengineer processes to achieve optimum workflow and productivity. Process-oriented change is often related to an organization's production process or how the organization assembles products or delivers services. Examples of process-oriented changes could be the adoption of robotics in a manufacturing plant, or of laser-scanning checkout systems at supermarkets (Chen et al., 2001).

★ *People-centered:* This type of change alters the attitudes, behaviours, skills or performance of employees in the company. Changing people-centered processes involves communicating, motivating, leading, and interacting within groups. This focus may entail changing how problems are solved, the way employees learn new skills, and even the very nature of how employees perceive themselves, their jobs, and the organization. Some people-centered changes may involve only incremental changes or small improvements in a process. For example, many organizations undergo leadership training that teaches managers how to communicate more openly with employees. Other programs may concentrate on team processes by teaching both managers and employees to work together more effectively to solve problems.

Levels of organizational change

There are five levels of change according to Dunphy and Stace (1993) that can occur in an organization, each of which is more difficult and needs more careful management.

1. Fine tuning

Most businesses are changing all the time in all kinds of ways, including refining policies, developing people, adjusting processes and so on. This is relatively easy and is often done without needing separate improvement or change projects. Nevertheless, even small changes can create surprising resistance and whilst the business change may be easy, care may need to be taken in deployment. There can also be a risk of 'butterfly wings' (in reference to the story of a butterfly that flaps its wings in the Amazon and tips air movement into a hurricane further north), so watching the overall system is key.

2. Incremental adjustment

Slightly larger than fine tuning, incremental adjustment to the organization can include correcting faulty processes, changing business emphasis, reallocating staff and so on.

This takes more work and has a greater risk of going wrong. It is more likely to use local improvement projects, where people take time out of their day work to engage in study of the situation and design of appropriate solutions.

Companies that do this often have internal facilitators who are trained in the methods of improvement and techniques of facilitating teams.

3. Process reengineering

Beyond incremental adjustment or improvement is 'Business Process Reengineering', or BPR, where the principle is that where incremental changes have limited effect, significant improvements may be achieved by forgetting how the process is enacted at the present and starting with a clean drawing board.

Such 'clean slate' approaches both liberate the designer to entirely rethink how things are done. On the other hand it might also lead to significant failure. A common failure in such projects is where a process gets automated but the software does not behave as well as intended.

4. Modular transformation

The next stage is to take an entire section of the business and re-think and re-build it, possibly in the re-engineering way but this time to be more efficient and perhaps re-direct the business into new products or markets.

Whilst reengineering may be done with the support of an external consultant, in modular transformation it is critical to engage external support from consultants, organizational psychologists and the like.

5. Corporate transformation

Corporate transformation involves major change that affects the whole company. Such levels of change may lead to mergers or acquisitions, where entire management layers are done away with, departments combined and so on. Another case is where a company has stagnated and seeks to transform itself for the modern age and new markets.

This is the most difficult form of change and is typically much harder than starting a company from scratch. Power battles that may certainly appear at lower levels escalate to a new level as directors' fight for their jobs, let alone the opportunity to build new empires.

A full change of this style may be many months in the preparation and take years to stabilize into normal working. It is expensive and is likely to require consultant and specialist support for a long period.

Levels of culture in change

According to Pritchett LP in their change management program dubbed *Business As Unusual: Change Essentials*, they provide the following levels of change that build change-adaptability as a core competency and move an organization to a new level.

Level 1 – *Cope* with change: Victim Mentality

A culture is operating at the first level of change when people primarily think in terms of just coping with the situation. They respond to change with a "victim mentality." You see a lot of helplessness and dependency behaviour. The general outlook is pessimistic. Too much valuable energy gets invested in resistance, anger, blamefulness, or fear. People focus on problems instead of solutions. They talk about how hard things are, and why they can't make it work. Usually the mindset at level one is that maybe change will pass. People wait and hope for a so-called "return to normal."

When a culture is stuck in the coping mode, people tend to slow down. They're overly cautious, too conservative, and many times this causes an organization to lose momentum. Naturally, productivity drops. Operating results take a hit. Employee energy and attention get diverted away from basic company business, and toward "me issues"—that is, concern over how one might be affected personally by the change.

When a culture lives at the first level of change, people try to protect the status quo. This means they make little effort to innovate, experiment, or take reasonable and appropriate risks. They hang on to the past instead of actively seeking to shape a better future. In the competitive game of business, they rely on defense and are lousy at playing the offense.

Overall, level one cultures are reactive, not proactive. It's the sort of culture that undermines both individual and organizational effectiveness.

Level 2 – *Comply* with change: Adjustment mentality

Cultures operating at the second level of change display more of an "adjustment mentality." Here at level two, there's a clear, but not impressive, effort made to comply with the situation. Employees may not like what's going on but they spend some energy accommodating the change. It may only be grudging compliance, or sort of a "cut your losses" attitude (accepting the inevitable), but they 'go with the flow'.

Nevertheless, these cultures are dangerously sluggish. The main problem, of course, is that people in level two fail to put forth the personal effort they should to help drive the change. They may have resigned themselves to what's going on, but they don't do all they should to bring about success. People go along but may grumble, and fail to function as effective change agents.

Cultures operating at level two fall way short of realizing their full potential. They're followers, not leaders, and have difficulty trying to compete.

Level 3 – *Capitalize* on change: Opportunity mentality

Cultures operating at the third level of change display an "opportunity mentality." Here the mindset is to capitalize on change. People try to turn it to their advantage. Instead of spending energy on resistance, they invest themselves in a search for positive benefits. Change is not only accepted, but also actively embraced as a potential opportunity that should be seized. The problem however is the culture is still in a reactive mode. However, at least people are looking for the bright side of things, though, with the idea that the cloud of change may have a silver lining. When change hits, they kick into gear and try to make the best of it.

In level three cultures, people align quickly with organization change. They readily contribute their energy and attention to the company's cause. These cultures are worthy competitors, but they leave a lot on the table.

Level 4 – *Create* change: Possibilities mentality

Cultures at level four are characterized by a "possibilities mentality." Overall, the organization is proactive, not reactive. Instead of waiting for change to happen, people set about to make it happen.

Level four cultures aren't content to cope with, comply with, or even exploit change—they create it. They do it to help the organization gain competitive advantage and be the architect of their own future. And because it's both energizing and fun, people operating as part of a level four culture are fired up by their work. They move with initiative, imagination, and a true sense of urgency. Here people have a sharp eye for new possibilities, for how things could be improved, for problems they can help fix. Level four outfits anticipate. They constantly scan for openings where change will give them an edge. The focus throughout is on operating results, on value creation, not merely on being busy or a hard worker.

The prevailing mindset in cultures at the fourth level of change is one of purpose, adventure, optimism, and faith. Here people invest themselves resourcefully in exploring, in experimenting and learning. They operate with a spirit of curiosity, a sense of mobility and pursuit and a hope for breakthroughs. They deliberately set forth to do things differently—to innovate—because they recognize change is their most promising solution. Level four cultures are fast, resilient, high-energy groups. Their flexibility and quick reflexes make them hard to outmaneuver.

These cultures are known for being trendsetters, for making the preemptive strike, for changing the game instead of merely trying to compete. Level four cultures don't fight the future. They partner with the world of tomorrow and co-create change.

CHAPTER REVIEW

Strategic change can be defined as "changes in the content of a firm's strategy as defined by its scope, resource deployments, competitive advantages, and synergy."

Change leadership is a "style of leadership in which the leader identifies the needed change, creates the vision to guide through inspiration, and executes the change with the commitment of the members of the group."

The four types of strategic change based on the classification of the extent of the change required, and the speed with which the change is to be achieved include: transformation, realignment, incremental change and big bang change.

For many organizations, the last decade has been fraught with restructurings, process enhancements, mergers, acquisitions, and layoffs – all in the hopes of achieving revenue growth, increased profitability and increased customer satisfaction. These changes have been classified as either being strategic, structural, process-oriented or people-oriented.

How organizations adapt to change as a core competency determines whether they stagnate or move successfully to a new level of growth and sustainability.

CHAPTER 3

The Role of Leadership in Strategic Change

Change leadership according to Fiona Graetz (2005) involves two roles:

1. Instrumental
2. Charismatic

While the two roles perform distinctive functions, they complement and strengthen each other.

Charismatic leadership is personalized leadership and is underpinned by strong interpersonal skills. It is crucial for envisaging, empowering, and energizing followers. On the other hand, the main elements of instrumental leadership are organizational design, control and reward which "involves managing environments to create conditions that motivate desired behaviour" (Nadler and Tushman, 1990, p.85), putting in place the enabling mechanisms that reinforce the required new values way of working.

Key dimensions of both the charismatic and instrumental roles include:

- Challenging the status quo and creating a "readiness for change" (Kouzes and Posner, 1995; Stata, 1992; Kotter, 1995; Tichy and Devanna, 1990).
- Inspiring a shared vision and personally communicating the fu-

ture direction with clear and honest answers to the what, why, and how questions. Not only must all employees in the organization "find the goal emotionally compelling", they must also clearly understand how they will contribute to achieving that goal (Jackson, 1997; Hamel and Prahalad, 1994).

- Creating additional sponsors at different levels of the organization, involving as many people as possible to build commitment.

- Enabling others to act by energizing, empowering, building teams, providing tangible support with appropriate resources, and putting in place the appropriate systems and structures.

- Symbolic and substantive actions using rewards and recognition to gain support; recognizing short-term gains or success stories to emphasize recognition of the new behaviours; and taking decisive action in identifying and addressing resistance (Jackson, 1997; Useem and Kochan, 1992; Kotter, 1995; Bertsch and Williams, 1994; Kanteretal, 1992; Johnson, 1992).

- Modelling the way by enacting the new behaviours in deeds as well as in words; personally demonstrating senior management involvement and commitment. The involvement of senior management is seen as fundamental to the success of the transformation process (Kotter, 1995; Stata, 1992; Stace and Dunphy, 1996; Kanter et..al.,1992; Nadleretal, 1995; Bertschand Williams, 1994; Blumenthal and Haspeslagh, 1994).

- With the help of key stakeholders, communicating the message repeatedly up, down and across the organization to ensure the momentum and enthusiasm for change is not diminished overtime.

- Communication by top management is seen as a powerful lever in gaining commitment and building consensus to required change. Successful implementation occurs in companies where executives "walk the talk", teaching new behaviours by example (Kouzes and Posner, 1995; Kotter, 1995; Kanter et.. al.,1992; Hambrick and Cannella,1989).

Leaders of change need to balance their efforts across all the three dimensions of an organizational change discussed below.

i. Managing interests – This can be through the form of mobilizing resources through influence, power and appropriate use of authority to bring about desired organizational change.

ii. Managing people emotions – Managing personal and people emotions is key to motivate and deal with conflicts that may come about during change. Change consumes a lot of mental and emotional energy and can easily stir up emotions and conflicts within self or with other people in the organizations. A leader must therefore provide an enabling environment which is possible when a leader is able to understand people psychology and their culture.

iii. Managing deliverables – An effective leader must be able to develop SMART objectives which will enable an organization realize its goals/mission. In any change initiative, a leader should have an "end in mind". This will help in developing targets and coordination of resources.

Role of management in change leadership

Leadership in times of change

The contingency theories of leadership show that leadership style and behaviour can vary according to the different characteristics of different organizational situations when it comes to leading change. These situations include the organization's stage of development, the nature of the change process itself and the forces for or against any change, including individuals' and groups, resistance to change.

There is little in literature to suggest which styles of leadership and behaviours are most associated with change. Transformational leadership however is associated with transformational or frame-breaking change. Research has shown that for organizations to go through transformational change at corporate level, a directive or coercive style of leadership is likely to be most successful (Dunphy, Stacy, 1993). Logic suggests that a more consultative style of management is more appropriate to incremental types of change that are, in turn, likely to be associated with environmental forces for change which are predictable and of moderate strength.

What a leader should do to make people adapt to change

Adaptive change is a sort of change that occurs when people and organizations are forced to adjust to a radically altered environment and which normally challenges the traditional understanding of the leader–follower relationship.

Leaders are shepherds, goes the conventional thinking, protecting their flock from harsh surroundings. The reality is however different. Leaders who truly care for their followers expose them to the painful reality of their condition and demand that they fashion a response. Instead of giving people false assurance that their best is good enough, leaders insists that people surpass themselves. And rather than smoothing over conflicts, leaders force disputes to the surface.

Adaptive change has emotional costs. Few people are likely to thank the leader for stirring anxiety and uncovering conflict. But leaders who cultivate emotional fortitude soon learn what they can achieve when they maximize their followers' well-being instead of their comfort.

To stay alive, Jack Pritchard had to change his life. Triple bypass surgery and medication could help, the heart surgeon told him, but no technical fix could release Pritchard from his own responsibility for changing the habits of a lifetime. He had to stop smoking, improve his diet, get some exercise, and take time to relax, remembering to breathe more deeply each day. Pritchard's doctor could provide sustaining technical expertise and take supportive action, but only Pritchard could adapt his ingrained habits to improve his long-term health. The doctor faced the leadership task of mobilizing the patient to make critical behavioural changes; Jack Pritchard faced the adaptive work of figuring out which specific changes to make and how to incorporate them into his daily life.

Companies today face challenges similar to the ones that confronted Pritchard and his doctor. They face adaptive challenges. Changes in societies, markets, customers, competition, and technology around the globe are forcing organizations to clarify their values, develop new strategies, and learn new ways of operating. Often the toughest task for leaders in effecting change is mobilizing people throughout the organization to do adaptive work.

Adaptive work is required when our deeply held beliefs are challenged, when the values that made us successful become less relevant, and when legitimate yet competing perspectives emerge. We see adaptive challenges every day at every level of the workplace—when companies restructure or reengineer, develop or implement strategy, or merge businesses. We see adaptive challenges when marketing has difficulty working with operations, when cross-functional teams don't work well, or when senior executives complain, "We don't seem to be able to execute effectively." Adaptive problems are often systemic problems with no ready answers.

Mobilizing an organization to adapt its behaviors in order to thrive in new business environments is critical. Without such change, any company today would falter. Indeed, getting people to do adaptive work is the mark of leadership in a competitive world. Yet for most senior executives, providing leadership and not just authoritative expertise is extremely difficult. Why? We see two reasons.

First, in order to make change happen, executives have to break a long-standing behavior pattern of their own: providing leadership in the form of solutions. This tendency is quite natural because many executives reach their positions of authority by virtue of their competence in taking responsibility and solving problems. But the locus of responsibility for problem solving when a company faces an adaptive challenge must shift to its people. Solutions to adaptive challenges reside not in the executive suite but in the collective intelligence of employees at all levels, who need to use one another as resources, often across boundaries, and learn their way to those solutions.

Second, adaptive change is distressing for the people going through it. They need to take on new roles, new relationships, new values, new behaviors, and new approaches to work. Many employees are ambivalent about the efforts and sacrifices required of them. They often look to the senior executive to take problems off their shoulders. But those expectations have to be unlearned. Rather than fulfilling the expectation that they will provide answers, leaders have to ask tough questions. Rather than protecting people from outside threats, leaders should allow them to feel the pinch of reality in order to stimulate them to adapt. Instead of orienting people to their current roles, leaders must disorient them so that new relationships can develop. Instead of quelling conflict, leaders have to draw the issues out. Instead of maintaining norms, leaders have to challenge "the way we do business" and help others distinguish immutable values from historical practices that must go.

Principles of change execution

Implementing change is both an art and science whereas executing change is a process, governed by a set of principles. According to Edmond Mellina (2002) leaders should adopt and approach change based on the following six guiding principles:

1. *Change is a three – phase process.* Change is about adopting new behaviours, developing fresh attitudes and doing things differently

    The first phase involves breaking the status quo – which makes people develop the perception of "false security" the so called "comfort zones". Any change initiative must start by applying disruptive forces to unfreeze (see page 40) the status quo. When a new CEO or a merger is announced, people expect change which must be initiated by the change leaders.

    In the transition phase, people disengage from the status quo and start to behave differently. The organization is in a state of limbo, between where it used to be and where it needs to go. Because of the instability, uncertainty and conflicts, people grow uncomfortable. They feel a loss of control and power and are tempted to return to the status quo.

A properly managed transition will result in ultimately reaching the desired state. However, the new way must be refrozen in order to become the norm.

2. *Major change requires an abyss and a lighthouse.* You won't change dramatically unless you have a strong purpose. Embarking on a transition always involves pain. The more drastic the change the more the pain.

The thought of plunging into an abyss gets people going, but does not point them in the light direction. People need a lighthouse, a reachable point holding the promise of less pain and more gain. The lighthouse guides people as they navigate the rough terrain of transition. People often decide to change because they start falling into an abyss. The many things they enjoy in life reinforce their drive to bounce back. These things represent their lighthouse.

3. *Each situation calls for a specific rate of change.* Each change initiative requires a specific tempo, which could range from a sprint to a marathon pace. The pace is varied depending on the sector or industry. Some entities require gradual approach whereas others are early adopters. Change leaders will however need to consider several factors to determine the right approach for example the first thing to analyze is the proximity and steepness of the abyss. If the organization is already slipping into the abyss, there is no choice but to act drastically. Commitment to change is then easier to build. It is a case of either change or die. The issue becomes whether it is too late to reverse the fall is. If the abyss is still at a distance or not clear to all, it will take more time, effort and patience to convince people of the danger. In addition, commitment to change shouldn't be generated too early; otherwise the initiative might lose steam halfway. Change leaders who fail to define their pace on these factors set themselves up for disappointment.

4. *Sponsorship is most often the cornerstone of the initiative.* Unless clearly anchored on the evolutionary side, the success of change effort will depend on the effectiveness and commitment of the sponsors.

The sponsorship constitutes the cornerstone of the initiative. If it is weak or stretched too thin, the probability of failure increases dramatically.

The sponsor has to decide what change to undertake, and then sanction it. The sponsor must have the power to do so. However, announcing the initiative in great fanfare is not enough. A sponsor must remain committed to the change, both publicly and privately.

During unfreezing (see page 41), supporting the effort requires building the case. The sponsor must communicate the danger of the abyss, paint a reachable lighthouse, and set realistic expectations about the difficulties involved in the transition.

During transition, the sponsor provides his or her agents with necessary support and resources (time, money, people) to implement the change successfully.

5. *Change is the game of proximity.* It is relatively easy to change the behaviours of few people working in the same environment. However, implementing change in larger, multi-location organizations is far more difficult. *Change cannot be mandated from a distance. It must be locally sponsored and locally managed.* The principle of proximity is driven by three considerations:

   i.   Successful implementation relies on effective, visible, sustainable and varied sponsorship.

   ii. People tend to resist change because it involves pain. In the absence of a local sponsor to reinforce commitment, change will fail.

   iii. Change is not an event, but a process. Like any complex process, it needs to be managed by competent people. If change is a game of proximity how should a large multi-location organization play? The answer is to create a domino-coalition of sponsors and change agents.

6. *Danger of taking a nap at the lighthouse.* Once the lighthouse is reached and the project looks complete, having dedicated so much energy to manage the transition, change agents are exhausted. Sponsors are anxious to launch other initiatives or to return to

their regular duties. However some people will have adopted the new behaviours merely out of fear and compliance. They constitute inactive pockets of resistance, ready to fight back whenever possible. People internalize change when it matches their interests and beliefs. Sponsors should make public new success stories. Finally, they should continue to take action against those who try to revive resistance.

Change is both an art and science. The six principles are the science. Leaders should learn them to guide their thinking and actions, while being adaptive in the implementation.

Roles and responsibilities of a change leader

The success of any organizational change rests in the hands of the change leader. People in the organization look up to and expect the change leader to plan, communicate, implement and guide them in order for the change initiative to be successful.

According to Gilley (2005), there are different roles and responsibilities that the leader must take if they are to qualify as an effective change leader.

Visionary

Leaders create and share visions. They make their visions the visions of the people that they lead. One responsibility of a leader is to challenge the status quo. Leaders look for opportunities and for challenges. They actively search for ways to change. The status quo represents complacency, mediocrity, and eventual decline – conditions that are unacceptable to most leaders. Leaders as visionaries imagine the future. Leaders have the ability to craft a mental picture of a state that does not exist yet. A vision of change portrays a vivid picture of the future. Leaders also develop a stewardship philosophy within the organization. True leaders put the welfare of their organizations and their members above their own. Lastly, as visionaries, leaders align the change with organizational vision, mission, strategy, as well as individual goals. Organizational vision should drive mission, which should drive strategy, which should drive individual goals. Thus, the appropriate change initiatives support the goals, strategy, mission and vision of the organization (Gilley 2005). Leadership during change also entails that the leader identifies innovative and creative ideas from the people in the organization. An effective leader always finds a way to change how things are done or develop the organization's products and services (Adair, 2004).

Inspirer

One of the most commonly cited traits of leaders is their ability to inspire others. Change leaders motivate and energize their constituents by meeting their needs; in other words, making the change personally beneficial in some meaningful way. Leaders sell change. Actively selling change involves identifying specific benefits valuable to each employee while concurrently minimizing potential losses or risks. Leaders also involve others in the change process. Involving employees at all levels of the organization proves powerfully motivating. Joint diagnosis of problems, potential solutions, and opportunities enables individuals feel ownership of the change along with feeling like worthy contributors to an important effort. Successful leaders live and model the change – they not only talk about the change, they enact it. They are the first to modify their behaviours, practice new ways, and advocate the benefits of change (Gilley, 2005).

Supporter

Enabling change involves communicating often, providing adequate resources and training, anticipating a learning curve, allowing for mistakes, rewarding individual and group change efforts, continually monitoring the process and its progress, making adjustments to the change effort as necessary, and celebrating milestones. Change leaders create a culture of change. Organizational culture reflects the shared beliefs, assumptions, and behaviours acquired over time by members of the firm.

Involving others – treating them like partners – conveys the sense that 'our success depends on this change'. Change leaders understand that individuals support what they help create. Since change involves engaging in something new, encouraging entrepreneurship, creativity, and innovation proves logical. In the supporter role, change leaders perfect the art of communication by interacting with employees at all levels and meeting their information and feedback needs (Williams, 2005).

Problem Solver

Effective change leaders analyze the situation and identify the problems. They also come up with creative solutions for those problems. Change leaders rely on their own investigation as well as their network of connected organizational members for data, insights, and feedback regarding the state of the environment surrounding the change (Williams, 2005).

Change Manager

Change management, by virtue of its complex nature, must be carefully monitored, lest the initiative gets out of control. The traditional definition of management is planning, directing, organizing and controlling (Gilley, 2005).

As change takes place in the organization, the leader must have the ability to create and sustain excellence. They must possess proactivity and a capacity for anticipatory thinking, envisioning and action. As a change manager a leader must recognize the importance of innovation and must have the skill to tap into all available sources of creativity. Lastly, the leader must integrate competence and the ability to co-ordinate the constituent parts and strengths of an organization into cohesive and effective production and delivery (Williams, 2005).

Leadership behaviours most relevant to change situations include the following:

- Communicates a clear and consistent vision (or plan) with commitment
- Champions change – able to engage others and get them ready (convince)
- Treats people with respect
- Demonstrates integrity and high ethical standards
- Sets and sustains high personal standards of delivery
- Is decisive, particularly when confronted with challenging issues
- Able to adapt and capitalize on new opportunities
- Builds effective relationships
- Builds effective team performance
- Openly encourages and recognizes the contribution of others
- Gives constructive feedback on a regular basis
- Encourages personal development and provides appropriate opportunities

CHAPTER REVIEW

The key dimensions of the charismatic and instrumental roles include:

- Creating a vision and setting direction
- Creating a capacity for change
- Leadership commitment
- Communicating the message
- Reinforcing the message and institutionalizing the new behaviours

The success of any organizational change rests in the hands of the change leader. To do this, the change leader must possess the following characteristics: be visionary, a problem solver, a change manager, people inspirer and supporter.

PART II

The Theory of Strategic Change

What's the use of running if you are not on the right road.
--German proverb

There is always a better strategy than the one you have; you just haven't thought of it yet.
--Sir Brian Pitman, former CEO of Lloyds TSB,
Harvard Business Review, April 2003

The whole problem with the world is that fools and fanatics are always so certain of themselves, but wiser people so full of doubts.
--Bertrand Russell 1872-1970,
English logician and philosopher

Unless a variety of opinions are laid before us, we have no opportunity of selection, but are bound of necessity to adopt the particular view which may have been brought forward.
--Herodotus, 5th century BC, Greek historian

The processes used to arrive at the total strategy are typically fragmented, evolutionary, and largely intuitive.
--James Quinn in Strategic Change: Logical Incrementalism, 1978

CHAPTER 4

Models of Strategic Change

There are several models or approaches that are capable of providing organizations with a robust, integrated and pragmatic approach to enable them understand the dynamics of the change process and then proactively drive organizational change.

MODELS OF ORGANIZATIONAL CHANGE

a) Lewin's Change Model

Kurt Lewin (1975) provided one of the early models of planned change. According to Lewin, in any individual, group or organization, there are two competing forces in operation. There are the forces of stability that aim to maintain the human system in the status quo and the forces of change that push the system towards change. These two forces are evenly balanced leading to a quasi-stationary equilibrium. This maintains a system in the status quo. For change to happen, therefore, either the forces of change need to be strengthened or the forces of stability need to be weakened. Change can be planned by altering the existing state, i.e., either by increasing the forces pushing for change or decreasing the forces maintaining the current state or applying a combination of both.

Organizational change can occur at three levels:

- *Individual* - change in an individual's attitudes, values, skills and behaviour
- *Structure and systems* - change in work design, reporting relationships, information systems, the reward systems, etc and
- *Organizational climate* - change in leadership style, interpersonal relations, decision-making style and other such aspects.

According to Lewin's model, the basis of change consists of three steps.

Unfreezing: this involves reducing forces maintaining an organization's/ individual behaviour at the present level. This may be accomplished at the individual level by sharing information revealing discrepancies between behaviour desired by the organizational members and the behaviour they currently exhibit; at the system level, by demonstrating the effectiveness of new designs such as matrix management and autonomous work teams; at the climate level, by the survey feedback methods to show how employees feel about certain management practices.

The purpose of unfreezing is to heighten the awareness of employees about the discrepancies currently prevailing in their behaviour, the systems, and the organizational climate, and attune them to the need for change. Because most people and organizations prefer stability and the perpetuation of the status quo, a successful change process must overcome the status quo by unfreezing old behaviours, processes, or structure. This approach includes the use of one-on-one discussions, presentations to groups, memos, reports, company newsletters, training programs, and demonstrations to educate employees about an imminent change and help them see the logic of the decision. Deficiencies in the current situation are identified and the benefits of the replacement are stressed.

Moving or changing: this refers to the shift in behaviour of an organization to a new level resulting in the developing of new behaviours, values and attitudes in individuals through changes in organizational structure and processes. The changes initiated must be perceived as solutions to the problem identified during the unfreezing stage. Change results from individuals being uncomfortable with the identified negative behaviours and being presented with new behaviours, role models, and support. In this phase, something new takes place in a system, and change is actually implemented. This is the point at which managers initiate change in such organizational targets as tasks, people, culture, technology, and structure. When managers implement change, people must be ready.

Refreezing: This is the stage where the organization, once the change has already taken place, stabilizes and achieves a new state of equilibrium and a preferred behaviour. It is often accomplished through the use of support mechanisms such as organizational culture, norms, policies, and structures, and reward systems aimed at reinforcing the new organizational state. Refreezing centers on reinforcing new behavior usually achieved through positive results, feelings of accomplishment or offering rewards. After management has implemented changes in organizational goals, products, processes, structures, or people, they cannot sit back and expect the change to be maintained over time. Behaviours that are positively reinforced tend to be repeated. In designing change, attention must be paid on how the new behaviours will be reinforced and rewarded.

b) Force-Field Analytic Problem Solving Model

This model was also developed by behavioural scientist Kurt Lewin in the 1940s. Since that time, the force-field analytic problem solving model has been widely used as a technique for encouraging groups of people to tackle organizational issues that previously seemed too complex or too deeply rooted to approach.

Force-field analysis – depicts the change process as one that must overcome a person's or organization's status quo or existing state of equilibrium that is, the balance between forces for change and forces that resist change. In any problem situation, the existing condition (status quo) has been reached because of a number of opposing forces. The change forces are known as drivers. (Drivers push toward a solution to the problem). When the strength of the drivers is approximately equal to the strength of the resisters, a balance or status quo is apparent. Until the relative strength of the force is changed, the problem will continue to persist.

When a change is introduced, some forces drive it and other forces resist it. To implement a change, management should analyze the change forces. By selectively removing forces that resist change, the driving forces will be strong enough to enable implementation. As resistant forces are reduced or removed, behaviour will shift to incorporate the desired changes.

To apply the model to a problem, a change leader should follow these steps:

1. *Carefully and fully specify the problem (status quo):* A problem may be defined as the difference between what currently exists and what should exist.

2. *Define objectives:* The change leader must consider what the situation will be like when it's solved.

3. *Brainstorm* to determine the driving and resisting forces that contribute to the problem.

4. *Analyze these forces more fully and develop a strategy:* This strategy should be aimed at strengthening the driving forces under the leader's control and weakening the resisting forces that they can realistically do something about.

5. *Compare strategy against company or departmental objectives:* The change leader must consider whether his or her problem-solving strategy will promote a change in the status quo.

c) Action Research Model

Action research represents another view of the organizational change process that is based on a research model. The researcher, normally the change agent, conducts an in-depth analysis, asking questions, interviewing, and evaluating records. Based on this diagnosis of the organizational situation, the change agent implements change using Lewin's three-state model (unfreezing, moving, and refreezing).

Lewin's concept of action research was that a human system, whether individual, group or an organization, can only be changed by engaging the human system in its own change. Lewin's action research empha- sized involvement and participation. He contended that involvement and participation of individuals facilitated their change arguing that inquiry and change in social systems could not be viewed as discrete activities. His famous dictum was: 'if you want to understand some- thing, try to change it'. In Lewin's original conception of action re- search, the agenda for change was set and driven by the researcher. A more recent argument is that change is expected to happen when indi- viduals reflect on their own mental models and choose to change them on their own free will, with the help and support of a change manager or leader (Nilakant and Ramnarayan, 2006).

Cummings and Huse (1989) further developed this model with eight main steps focusing on the planned change activity as a cyclical pro- cess. Initial research about the organization is undertaken which pro- vides the requisite information to guide further action. The results of the action are assessed once again to provide information to guide fur- ther action. The cycle repeats as an ongoing process.

The eight steps are illustrated below:

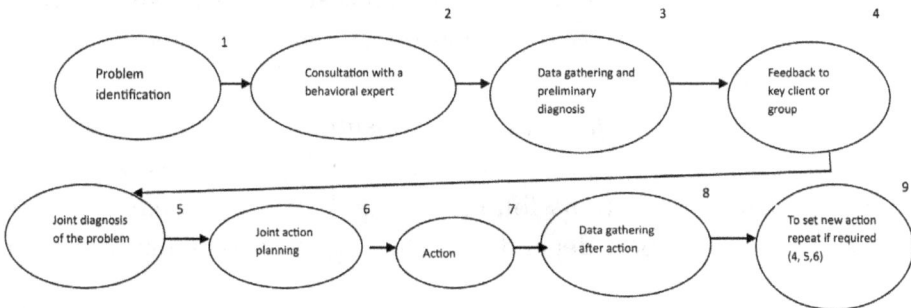

Figure 3: Action Research Model

The action research model is cyclical in nature; new data is again gath- ered after the action has been taken to measure and determine the effects of the action. The feedback is obtained. The situation is re-diagnosed and new action taken.

This model is helpful for organizations to implement planned change and develop general knowledge (to apply in future scenarios).

1. *Problem identification:* Here, key executives identify the existence of one or more problems to alleviate with organizational development practitioner.

2. *Consultation with a behavioural expert:* Problem sensed; The leaders realize that the problem can be solved with an organizational development expert.

3. *Data gathering and preliminary diagnosis:* The consultant and the members of the organization gather data with the help of:
   - Interviews
   - Process observations
   - Questionnaires
   - Analysis of organizational performance data

4. *Feedback to key client group:* The client gets the data; strengths and weaknesses of the area studied and determined. The consultant provides the client all relevant and useful data.

5. *Joint diagnosis of the problem:* The entire group discusses the feedback; additional research is summarized and submitted to the groups for validation, further diagnosis, identification of the problem.

6. *Joint action planning:* The consultant and the management team jointly agree on problem solving methods; analyzed, alternative actions found out; the best action selected. The specific action depends on the organization's environment and other factors:
   - Cultural
   - Technological
   - Work environment

- Problem(s) to be resolved
- Time
- Costs

This depends on the desired organizational development (OD) intervention on the above.

7. ***Action:*** Involves actual change from one organizational state to another; it may include:

    ❑ Installing new methods and procedures

    ❑ Recognizing structures and work designs

    ❑ Reinforcing new behaviour

8. ***Data gathering after action:*** Model is cyclic in nature; New data is again gathered after the action; get the feedback; situation is re-diagnosed and new action taken.

d) Planning Model

This model was developed by Lippit, Watson and Westley in 1958 as a tool for bringing about planned change in organizations. It was then modified by Kolb and Frohman in 1970. The model is based on the principle that information must be freely and openly shared between the organization and the change agent and must be able to be translated into action.

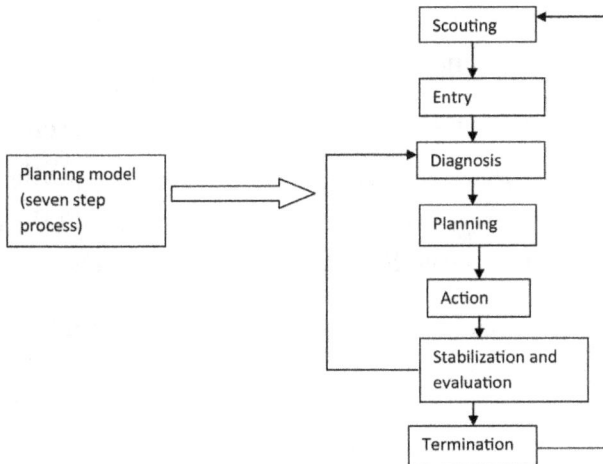

Figure 4: Planning Model (Seven Step Process)

45

1. *Scouting:* The change agent and the organization jointly explore the need and areas requiring change.

2. *Entry:* The development of mutual contact and mutual expectations.

3. *Diagnosis:* The stage where specific improvement goals are identified.

4. *Planning:* The stage where actual and possible reasons for resistance to change are identified to planning for specific improvement of goals.

5. *Action:* The implementation of the steps identified in the planning stage.

6. *Stabilization and evaluation:* A phase where evaluation is undertaken to determine the extent of success of the planned change and the need for further action or termination.

7. *Termination:* A phase where a decision is made to leave the system or to end and begin another.

The change agent and management can modify the above sequential phase. The strategies and approaches can be modified depending on the diagnosis and re-diagnosis of the problem as indicated by the feedback arrows.

e) Integrative Model of Planned Change

Bullock and Batten in 1985 developed this model. The basis of this integrative model of planned change is on the following thinking:

•   An organization exists in different states at different times.

•   Phased movement can occur from one state to another.

•   An understanding of both the temporal states and the change processes needed to move from one state to another.

The four stages involved in the sequence are listed and explored further below:

i.   Exploration phase

ii.   Planning phase

iii.   Action phase

iv.   Integration phase

i)   Exploration process – stage 1

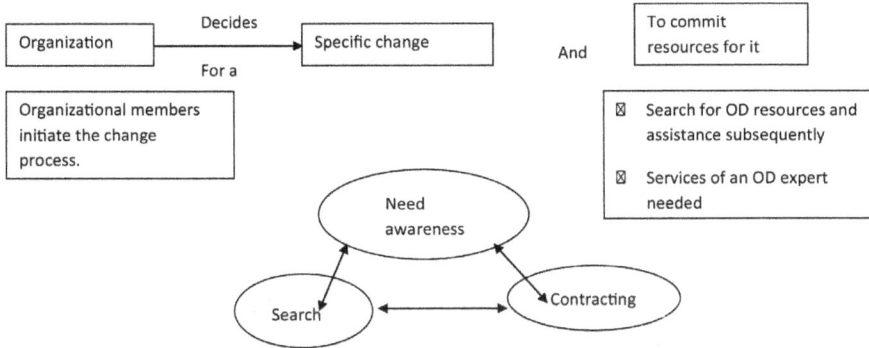

Figure 5: Exploration Process – Bullock and Batten Model

ii)   Planning phase – stage 2

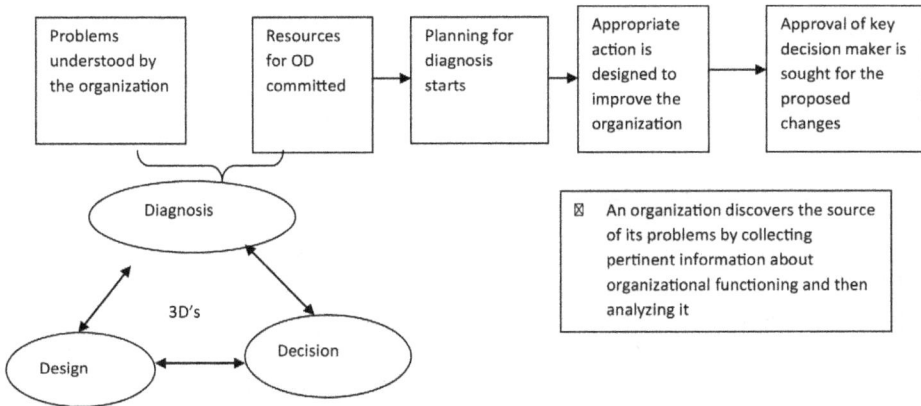

Figure 6: Planning Phase – Bullock and Batten Model

Diagnosis is jointly undertaken by organization members and experts; goals are set for the change effort; appropriate action is designed to improve the organization; approval of key decision makers is sought for the proposed changes.

iii)   Action phase – stage 3

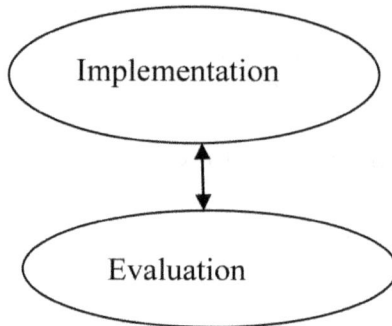

Figure 7: Action Phase – Bullock and Batten Model

The changes derived from planning are implemented (includes processes aimed at transitioning the organization from its current state to the desired future state). The change activities are then monitored and evaluated periodically to assess their progress and check whether positive results are being achieved or whether they need modification and refinement.

iv)   Integration phase – stage 4

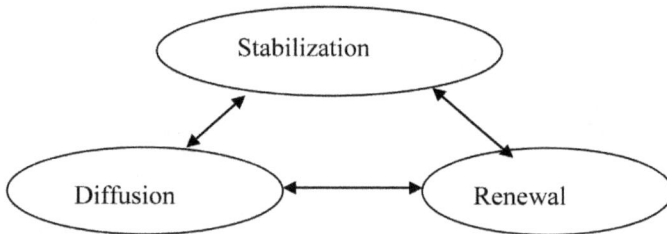

Figure 8: Integration Phase – Bullock and Batten Model

This involves making the changes part of regular organizational functioning after having successfully implemented and stabilized them. The diffusion and renewal activities would follow as the new behaviour is reinforced through feedback, incentives and rewards. Finally, the contract with the OD professional is gradually terminated.

CHAPTER REVIEW

The models of organizational change include the following:

a) **Lewin's Change Model:** According to Lewin's model, the basis of change consists of three steps: Unfreezing, moving or changing and refreezing.

b) **Force-Field Analytic Problem Solving Model:** This model was also developed by behavioural scientist Kurt Lewin and depicts the change process as one that must overcome a person's or organization's status quo or existing state of equilibrium that is, the balance between forces for change and forces that resist change.

c) **Action Research Model:** Action research represents another view of the organizational change process that is based on a research model. The researcher, normally the change agent, conducts an in-depth analysis, asking questions, interviewing, and evaluating records.

d) **Planning Model:** The model is based on the principle that information must be freely and openly shared between the organization and the change agent and must be able to be translated into action.

e) **Integrative Model of Planned Change:** Bullock and Batten in 1985 developed this model. The basis of this model is on the thinking that an organization exists in different states at different times, that phased movement can occur from one state to another and that an understanding of both the temporal states and the change processes needed to move from one state to another is required for success. The four stages involved in the sequence are exploration phase, planning phase, action phase and integration phase.

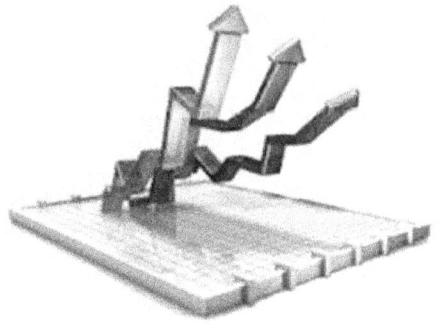

CHAPTER 5

Dimensions of Strategic Change

No firm can escape change! Change management is a new discipline that focuses on why and how organizations change. A major finding in change management research is that most organizations do not manage change well.

Change management is managing the process of implementing major changes in information technology, business processes, organizational structures and job assignments to reduce the risks and costs of change and optimize its benefits.

As societies continue to evolve and changing demand creates the need for new products and services, businesses often are forced to make changes to stay competitive. The businesses that continue to survive and even thrive are usually the ones that most readily adapt to change. A variety of factors can cause a business to reevaluate its methods of operation (Chris Joseph, n.d.).

Business and non-business organizations confront the world that is challenging in several ways. Managers face five major challenges:

1. Competition

That is, increased competition for an organization's resource. Business organizations face increased competition in their markets and for their inputs. Non-business organizations on the other hand face competition for their funds.

Organizations have to compete in the world which is constantly changing in the aspects of:

- Globalization
- Technological changes
- Unanticipated events (uncertain and unpredictable)
- An empowered and knowledgeable customer who is sensitive to quality, freshness and responsive to changing lifestyle.

The future impact of a new technology may be hard to predict; in a globalized market place, competition may arise from anywhere; new legislation that impacts business may emerge; internal uncertainties are also found within the organization – prediction of how people would react to change; people exit from companies for better pay, career, lifestyle or working conditions; individual jockeying for power. Thus a manager's job has become both challenging and difficult.

The entrance of a new competitor into a market can cause a business to change its marketing strategy. For example, a small electronics store that was the only game in town might have to change its image in the marketplace when a large chain store opens nearby. While the smaller store might not be able to compete in price, it can use advertising to position itself as the friendly, service-oriented local alternative.

2. Technology

Innovations in technology can force a business to change just to keep up. Employees who have never used computers need to be trained to operate the new computer system. A business also can benefit by implementing a technological change. For example, an airline can introduce email ticketing which can result in increased efficiency and better customer service while meeting little customer resistance.

3. Desire for Growth

Businesses that want to attain growth might need to change their method of operations. For example, in the USA, the Subway sandwich chain started as a small business under a different name in 1965 and struggled through its first several years. The company began to flourish after it changed its name to Subway in 1974 and began to sell franchises (there were 22,525 Subway franchise units in the United States alone as of 2009, www.entreprenuer.com).

4. Need to Improve Processes

A business might need to implement new production processes to become more efficient and eliminate waste. In 2003, Cigna Healthcare implemented a leaner production process known as Six Sigma to improve service and reduce operating costs. In 2006, the company was recognized by the J.D. Power independent rating organization for its high level of service and quality.

5. Government Regulations

Changes in government regulations can have an impact on how a company does business. Newly mandated safety procedures can force a factory to change its production process to create a safer work environment. Businesses that make or distribute consumer goods such as food products might have to add more quality control measures to ensure consumer safety. Examples in Kenya include The NTSA Act regulating movement of public service vehicles at night and the VAT Act.

The key dimensions of change management

The figure below shows some of the key dimensions of change management, and the level of difficulty, time to resolve and the business impact involved. The people, process and technology factors involved in the implementation of business/IT strategies and applications, or other changes caused by introducing new information technologies into a company.

		Technology	Process	People
High / Impact on business / **Low**	**Strategic**	Enterprise architecture Supplier partnership Systems integrators Outsourcing	Ownership Design Enterprise wide processes Internet enterprise processes	Change leaders Loose/tight controls Executive sponsorship and support Aligning conditions on satisfaction
	Operational	Technology selection Technology support Installation requirements	Change control Implementation Management support processes	Recruitment Retention Training Knowledge transfer

Low ————————————————————————→ High

Level of Difficulty/Time to Resolve

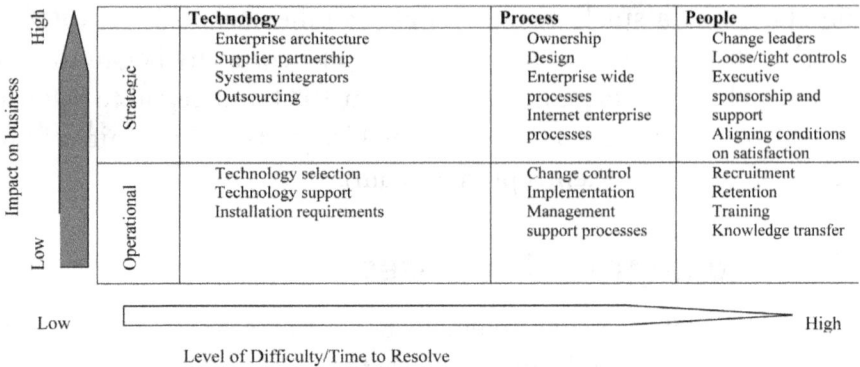

Figure 9: The Key Dimensions of Change Management

System integrators are consulting firms or other outside contractors who may be paid to assume the responsibility for developing and implementing a new e-business application, including designing and leading its change management activities.

People are a major focus of organizational change management. This includes activities such as developing innovative ways to measure, motivate and reward performance. It is people who will ultimately cause the change to be a success or a failure. The implications of change on individuals are important without which we can never really hope to manage large scale effectively.

Most of today's work is done by forming teams. This needs team collaboration and team work for it to succeed. Another important aspect of change management is the crucial role of leadership.

Change management therefore involves:
   ❊   Individual, team and organizational change
   ❊   The leadership of change

The implementation includes:
   ❊   Application
   ❊   Restructuring
   ❊   Mergers and acquisition
   ❊   Cultural change
   ❊   IT based process change

The change management process

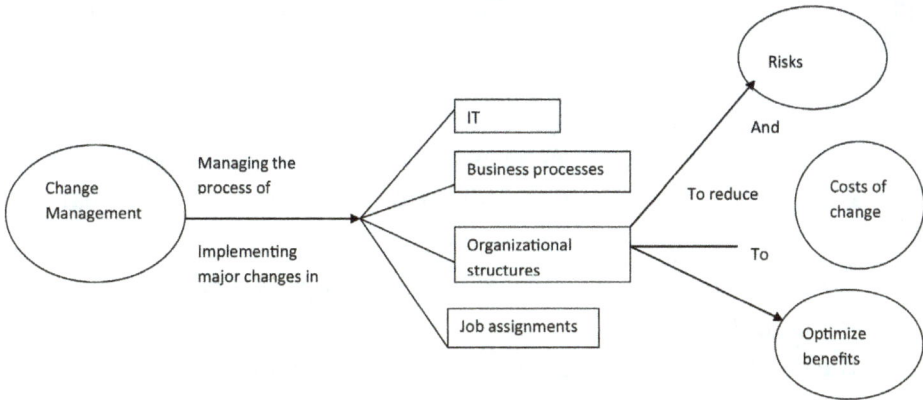

Figure 10: The Change Management Process

Forces of change

There are two sets of change forces that affect an organization: the internal and external environment. These forces are discussed in detail below.

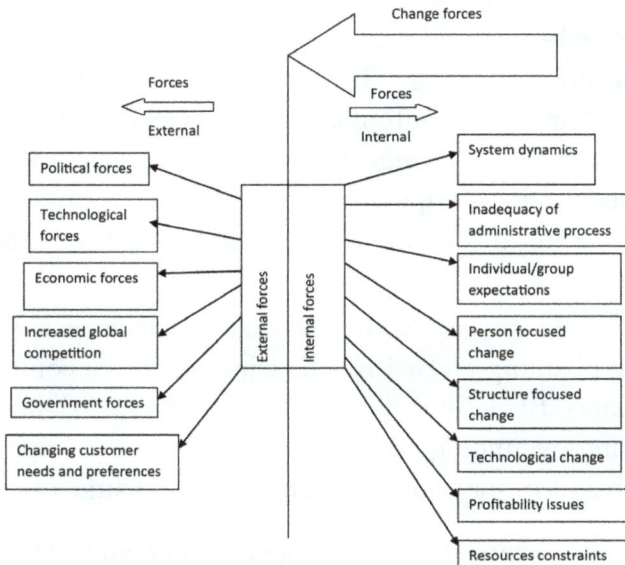

Figure 11: Forces of Change

THE INTERNAL ENVIRONMENT

The internal environment of change could be influenced by the following factors:

a. *System dynamics:* An organization is made up of sub systems similar to that of the super personalities in the human brain which go on interacting with each other creating changes in human behaviour.

b. *Administrative processes:* As the time progresses, the revision of goals and objectives in an organization takes place, resulting in the changes in existing rules, procedures and regulations.

c. *Individual or group expectations:* Man is a social being whose needs and desires keep on changing. This brings differing expectations among individuals and groups. Positive factors: one's ambition, need to achieve, career growth, capabilities etc. The negative aspects include: one's fears, insecurities, frustrations etc.

d. *Structure-focused change:* A change that alters any of the basic components of an organization structure or overall design (to reduce costs, increase profitability), for instance downsizing, decentralization, job redesign etc. Global competition has made many companies to act mean and lean.

e. *Technological:* A change that impacts the actual process of transforming input to output is known as technological change. For example, equipment change, work process, information processing, work sequence, Computer Aided Designs/ Computer Aided Manufacturing (CAD/CAM), Robotics, Point of Sales (POS), internet etc.

f. *Person focused change:* A change that is concerned with human resource planning and with enhancing employee competence and performance. Structural change in terms of expansion, contraction or resizing, technological input – all these have implications for human resource management. The focused changes are as under:

 ✦ Replacement: when employees further training does not help.

 ✦ Replacement: where an employee's current training is best suited.

✦ Employee training and development.

✦ Laying down new recruitment and selection policies in tune with changing technologies.

g. *Resource constraints:* Resources here could be money, material, personnel, machinery, information technology – depletion, inadequacy or non-availability of the above force organization to change.

Internal Triggers for change

Examples of internal triggers for change may include:

➔ An organization becoming unionized or de-unionized

➔ A new chief executive or other senior managers

➔ A revision of administrative structure

➔ The redesign of a group of jobs

➔ The redesign of a factory or office layout

➔ The purchase of a new IT equipment

➔ A new business or marketing strategy

➔ A cut in overtime working

➔ Staff redundancies

➔ Strengthening of specific departments such as research and development

EXTERNAL FORCES OF CHANGE

The following six forces of change are due to the external environment.

1. **Political forces:** Regardless of a country's political ideology-Marxist, dictatorship or democracy- its policies, laws and actions have a profound effect on the world of business. Political factors that trigger change include: government legislations, political ideology, international law, universal rights, wars, local regulations, taxation and trade union activities.

    Not only do changes in the political environment influence organizations directly, they also interact with changes in the economic environment such as the government-inspired privatization of state corporations and the formation of regional trading blocs like COMESA and East African Cooperation have an impact on a country's economic environment. Changes coming from one sector of the environment are compounded by their interaction with influencing factors from other sectors of the environment which is a clear demonstration that environmental triggers for change rarely act as single influencers.

As government policies, laws and actions affect organizations and people's everyday lives, so do the attitudes and expectations of people towards work, in the context of other aspects of their lives. Socio-cultural factors that influence the way organizations are set up, run and managed as well as their capacity to attract people to work within them are many. These include the following: demographic trends of customers and employees, lifestyle changes, skills availability, attitudes to work and employment, attitudes to minority groups, gender issues, willingness and ability to move, concern for the environment and business ethics.

The changes that happened in Germany (unification of the East and the West), as well as in the other nations of east European countries to democracy and market economy, and also in USSR (Russia), the Gulf war, crisis in Yugoslavia and the current happenings in China are good examples of political upheavals that necessitated change in other nations which are well knitted with them.

2. **Economic forces**: The uncertainty about future trends in the economy is a major cause of change. Many countries are undergoing changes in declining productivity, inflation, deflation, interest rates, capital investment, petrol prices, lower consumer confidence, recessions etc. These have a marked impact on different economies and on organizations.

3. **Technological forces**: Dramatic technological shifts are taking place in all nations globally. Technological advancements (especially in the IT field i.e. computer and communications, information systems, internet technologies including social media) are found everywhere and have revolutionalized the work place. New

quality products are rolling out, improved services are being provided and costs have dramatically reduced. For example desktop computers, TVs, laptops and even smart phones prices have significantly gone down. In addition, communication costs have been slashed. Advances in technology have contributed to the development of economies. Bio-chemical and bio-medical technologies are replacing several technologies especially in medicine, agriculture and industry.

4. **Government forces**: Government interventions in the form of regulations also lead to change. Some examples of government interventions could be in deregulation, foreign exchange, antitrust laws, antidumping duties, suspension agreements, protectionism etc.

5. **Increased global competition**: Companies have to operate globally for survival and growth. Automobile industries are competing globally to retain competitive edge. Companies have gone virtual by establishing strategic alliances. No single company can survive on their own unless it ties up with other companies. Examples of relationship enterprises include those of IBM, Toyota, Toshiba etc. Airlines have also built such alliances for example that of KQ and KLM. Dynamic multi-venturing is a new mantra. Many a times, even arch-rivals have also come together to work on a common product goal.

6. **Changing customer needs and preferences**: Organizations are innovating and bringing new products continually to meet the customer needs and preferences which are changing quite often. Good examples are products from Sony, Samsung, Apple etc.

CHAPTER REVIEW

An organization is a system receiving inputs from its environment and releasing outputs back into it. Social and technological changes have impacted on the products and services offered by organizations and the way they operate. An organization's environment includes broader influences such as the internationalization of trade, influences from the political environment, the prevailing political ideology, the general economic situation, attitudes to trade unions, change from public to private ownership and vice versa, demographic changes and changes in family structure as well as differences between the rich and the poor. Examples of triggers for change from changes in technology and the economic environment are many and varied. Technological factors influencing change include: information technology and the use of internet, new production processes, computerization of processes and changes in transport technology. Economic factors influencing change in organizations include: competitors, suppliers, currency exchange rates, employment rates, wage rates, government economic policies, other countries' economic policies, lending policies of financial institutions and changes from public to private ownership.

Managers must contend with all factors that affect their organizations and encourage change.

The **external environment** is affected by political, social, technological, and economic stimuli outside of the organization that cause changes.

The **internal environment** on the other hand is affected by the organization's management policies and styles, systems, and procedures, as well as employee attitudes.

The forces of change from the external environment include:
* Regulatory changes that organizations must comply with.
* Sudden economic shocks leading to transformational change.
* Social changes.
* Technological developments.

The internal forces that can bring about change include:
⊙ A continuous reaction to historical changes.
⊙ Innovation - the company may develop a new product or a new manufacturing process.
⊙ Individual executives' ambition.
⊙ The pursuit of growth.

CHAPTER 6

Developing Strategic Thinking Capabilities

Strategic thinking refers to cognitive processes required for the collection, interpretation, generation, and evaluation of information and ideas that shape an organization's sustainable competitive advantage (Hughes and Beatty, 2005). In other words, for organizations to develop sustainable competitive advantage, it's not enough to have great individual strategic thinkers. It also takes individuals who influence one another's thinking, deepening and enhancing their collective understanding and insight. This is because the complex and changing nature of the competitive environment increasingly requires bringing diverse perspectives to bear on business challenges.

Hughes and Beatty (2005) identified five strategic thinking competencies that they believe are integrally embedded in the broader challenge of strategic leadership and typically least developed. These strategic thinking competences are:

1. Scanning
2. Visioning
3. Reframing
4. Making common sense
5. Systems thinking

Scanning

Though the strategic learning process can actually begin anywhere, it typically begins with assessing where the organization is. This involves examining the organization's current strategic situation, and it includes an analysis of the opportunities and threats in the industry as well as the strengths and weaknesses inside the organization what is commonly called a SWOT analysis;

❋ *Strengths:* What internal capabilities or assets give the organization a competitive advantage? In what ways does the organization serve its key internal and external stakeholders well?

❋ *Weaknesses:* What internal capabilities or assets is the organization relatively ineffective or inefficient at performing or possessing, or so limited in capacity as to put it at a competitive disadvantage? In what ways does the organization fall short in serving key internal and external stakeholders?

❋ *Opportunities:* What conditions or possible future conditions in the external environment might give the organization a competitive advantage and enhance achievement of its vision if taken advantage of?

❋ *Threats:* What conditions or possible future conditions in the external environment might put the organization at a competitive disadvantage and inhibit achievement of its vision if steps are not taken to minimize their impact?

According to Hughes and Beatty (2005), for the individual manager, scanning as a strategic thinking competency involves attending to the informational horizon beyond one's own job, team, division, function, company, or even industry.

Good strategic thinkers:

1. Scan their environments for data, trends, or ideas that could potentially have significance for their organization's future competitiveness.

2. Scan diverse sources of information, such as magazines and journals outside their business or industry literature. They

seek out perspectives from others involved in diverse kinds of work. They can sift through information quickly, not necessarily deeply but with an eye for the anomalous or otherwise interesting bit of data.

Visioning

A vision represents a view of what the organization (or a department, group, or other unit) can and should become. There can be formal expressions of organizational aspiration, as in official vision statements or core values. At the same time, however, many individuals also hold personal but unspoken versions of organizational aspirations. Unfortunately, they seldom share these personal visions. Knowing the different implicit aspirations individuals have for their organization can be informative and even inspiring.

It is sometimes said that vision must come from the top. Hughes and Beatty (2005) recommend that brainstorming sessions with members of the organization can enrich the vision-setting process. This is because it affords broader opportunity for people to share personal versions of aspirations for the organization. It also can inform people throughout the organization of the many different possibilities and visions that can exist simultaneously (not necessarily inconsistently) within one organization. It can also generate collective inspiration for an organization's future, even amid differing individual versions of it.

Reframing

Reframing involves the ability to see things differently, including new ways of thinking about an organization's strategic challenges and basic capabilities. It involves questioning or restating the implicit beliefs and assumptions that are often taken for granted by organization members. The process often uses metaphors such as

- Leadership as combat
- Leadership as sport
- Leadership as art

- Leadership as a machine
- Leadership as gardening

Reframing can be an essential part of resolving an organizational dilemma, but it also can be experienced as unhelpful and disruptive to those who may not perceive any dilemma.

Some reframing questions a leader might want to ask could be:

1. What would we do differently if we *really* listened to our customers?

2. What are some different ways we can think about what *quality* means in our work?

3. What could we be the best in the world at doing? How might doing that change the nature of our organization?

4. Instead of thinking about ourselves as an organization that [fill in how you currently characterize your work], what if we thought about ourselves as an organization that [fill in a different way of thinking about what your organization does].

5. Have certain processes and activities in our organization merely become ends in themselves rather than means to an end?

6. Ask yourself, "Is our structure serving our strategy, or is our strategy serving our structure?"

7. Use the idea of the inverted pyramid organization as a metaphor (that is, instead of thinking of the senior leaders at the top of the pyramid and being "served by" everyone else in the organization, think about senior leaders as the bottom of the pyramid and serving everyone else). What else might it be helpful to "turn upside down"?

Research on decision making indicates that how decisions are framed makes a significant difference in the decisions made. Explore alternative ways of framing the problem to see whether that makes a difference in the relative attractiveness or apparent desirability of the options.

Making Common Sense

One of the most important things leaders do—especially strategic leaders—is to help others in their organizations make sense of the world around them, the challenges they collectively face, and how they will face them together. Strategic leadership requires making common sense amid complex and ambiguous conditions. The dynamic challenges facing organizations today contribute to a common experience of lack of clarity about direction and alignment, and a sense of disorganization and confusion. Strategic leadership involves making common sense amid such chaotic conditions. It involves giving some coherence to what could otherwise feel like confusing and contradictory communications and signals at work.

Developing shared understanding is important because people often rely on implicit knowledge rather than on explicit knowledge when it comes to communicating or sharing ideas. Unarticulated knowledge can cause people to feel unclear or confused about the apparent disconnectedness between the priorities, policies, and processes of different teams, departments, or divisions in their organization. This is less likely to happen when people share a common understanding of their vision and strategy.

Some examples of what people need to make common sense about at work include:

- Their vision of the future
- Their understanding of challenges facing the organization
- Guidance from higher authority
- How the team will interface with other individuals and groups
- Obstacles to group or team success, and ways to overcome them

Systems Thinking

Effective strategic thinkers are able to discern the interrelationships among different variables in a complex situation. For example, they might wonder what would happen to sales of a product if the price to consumers was reduced. Or what would happen to sales if marketing was increased? If these variables operated in a simple linear fashion, then either choice would increase sales. But if they represented variables in a complex and dynamic system (as is more often the case), then the results would be less predictable. For example, if product quality was an important component of product attractiveness for consumers, then a decrease in price might be perceived as an indicator of poor product quality and consequently slow sales, no matter what was spent on marketing.

Systems thinking can help you better understand complex problems like these, so it's an important tool for your strategic thinking toolkit.

Hughes and Beatty (2005) offer five tactics for better systems thinking which are discussed in detail below.

1. Look for patterns over time
2. Look at the big picture
3. Look for complex interactions
4. Hypothesize key causal relationships
5. Validate your understanding of "what causes what"

Long-Term Patterns. People's usual approach to things in most spheres of life can be characterized by what we call *static thinking*. With static thinking, little attention tends to be given to "how we got here," and equally little attention tends to be given to "how we'll get from here to there."

Dynamic thinking, by contrast, examines how key variables brought a system to its present state (and may be keeping it there), and it uses understanding of the past to guide future initiatives.

This emphasis upon understanding pathways is important, since undue focus on current conditions tends to be associated with assumptions of linear trajectories from the past to the present and from the present to the future.

The Big Picture. Big-picture thinking involves seeing at each level how the different parts of a system operate as a whole (for example at the facility, regional, and enterprise levels). And big-picture thinking at each level is not possible using the detailed quantitative analysis of parts (functions, departments, divisions, silos, and so on) that is ubiquitous in organizations today.

Complex Interactions. Understanding that the appearance of simple causal relationships often masks complex interactions among unpredictable variables can alert you to the possibility of the unintended consequences of your actions.

Key Causal Relationships. Strategy is about trade-offs: choosing to do this rather than that, choosing to be this rather than that, choosing to develop one capability over another. By its nature, a good strategy is not all things to all people. A good strategy is clearly centered on a few key priorities. The strategic challenge for any organization is to integrate understanding of its aspirations, strengths, and weaknesses with understanding of its competitive environment in order to identify the two or three critical leverage points that bring success. These are the key strategic drivers.

Understanding What Causes What. It's important for leaders in organizations to confirm their theory of the business. People, including leaders, have a tendency to look for information that will confirm what they believe (or "know to be true") rather than to look more intentionally for information that could disconfirm their preconceptions.

The danger in organizations is that if people look only for signs that they are on the right path (that their theory of the business is valid), they can often find them. But if they do not also look for signs that they are wrong, they will miss critical information.

CHAPTER REVIEW

Strategic thinking refers to cognitive processes required for the collection, interpretation, generation, and evaluation of information and ideas that shape an organization's sustainable competitive advantage. Hughes and Beatty (2005) identified five strategic thinking competencies that they believe are integrally embedded in the broader challenge of strategic leadership and typically least developed. These strategic thinking competencies that will enhance your effectiveness as a strategic leader are:

- Scanning
- Visioning
- Reframing
- Making common sense
- Systems thinking

PART III

The Practice of Strategic Change

> However beautiful the strategy, you should occasionally look at the results.
> --Sir Winston Churchill 1874-1965, English statesman

> Unless a variety of opinions are laid before us, we have no opportunity of selection, but are bound of necessity to adopt the particular view which may have been brought forward.
> --Herodotus, 5th century BC, Greek historian

> In real life, strategy is actually very straightforward. You pick a general direction and implement like hell.
> --Jack Welch in Winning, 2005

> How many senior executives discuss the crucial distinction between competitive strategy at the level of a business and competitive strategy at the level of an entire company?
> --C.K. Prahalad and Gary Hamel, in their article: The core competence of the corporation, 1990

> I claim not to have controlled events, but confess plainly that events have controlled me.
> --Abraham Lincoln 1809-1865, sixteenth American president

> Perception is strong and sight weak. In strategy it is important to see distant things as if they were close and to take a distanced view of close things.
> --Miyamoto Musashi 1584-1645, legendary Japanese swordsman

> Do not repeat the tactics which have gained you one victory, but let your methods be regulated by the infinite variety of circumstances.
> --Sun Tzu c. 490 BC, Chinese military strategist

CHAPTER 7

Organizational Culture & Strategic Change

Change and Organization Dynamics

I t has been argued that when an organization is facing a planned change, the biggest challenge is to manage the dynamics not the pieces. Included in the dynamics, are the prevailing beliefs, behaviours and assumptions that each member acquires over time. In other words, consideration and emphasis must be made on the organization's culture. Culture according to Kotter (1996) refers to norms of behaviour and shared values among a group of people. Norms are common or pervasive ways of acting that are found in a group and that persist because group members tend to behave in ways that teach these practices to new members, rewarding those who fit in and giving sanctions to those who do not. Shared values are important concerns and goals shared by most of the people in a group that tend to shape group behaviour and that often persist over time, even when group membership changes. Culture is shared, providing cohesiveness among people throughout an organization, and developed over time. An organization's existing culture is the product of beliefs, behaviours, and assumptions that have in the past contributed to success. Conner (1992) defines organizational culture as the interrelationship of shared beliefs, behaviours, and assumptions that are acquired over time by members of an organization (cited in Gilley and Maycunich 2000, p. 284). The prevailing beliefs, behaviours and assumptions of an organization guide what are considered appropriate or inappropriate actions in which individuals and groups engage. An organization's collective beliefs, behaviours and assumptions affect daily business decisions, actions and operations on two levels, overt and covert. The overt level represents observable, intentional, and direct influences on operations. The covert level is characterized by obscure, unintentional, and indirect influences on operations. These latter influences are difficult to change because employees are often unaware of them. On the overt level, an organization operates on beliefs and observable behaviours. At the covert level, the organization is influenced by employees' collective assumptions. These combine to influence oral and written communications, organizational structure, power and status, policies and procedures, compensation and reward systems, and the design and use of physical facilities (Gilley and Maycunich, 2000).

Organizational change, particularly changes in organizational culture can be very challenging and problematic. Organizational culture is difficult to change because it is deeply embedded in the shared behaviours of organization members and working relationships, which have developed over time. The culture of the organization defines appropriate behaviour, bonds and motivates individuals and asserts solutions where there is uncertainty. Organizational culture functions at all levels, from subconscious to visible.

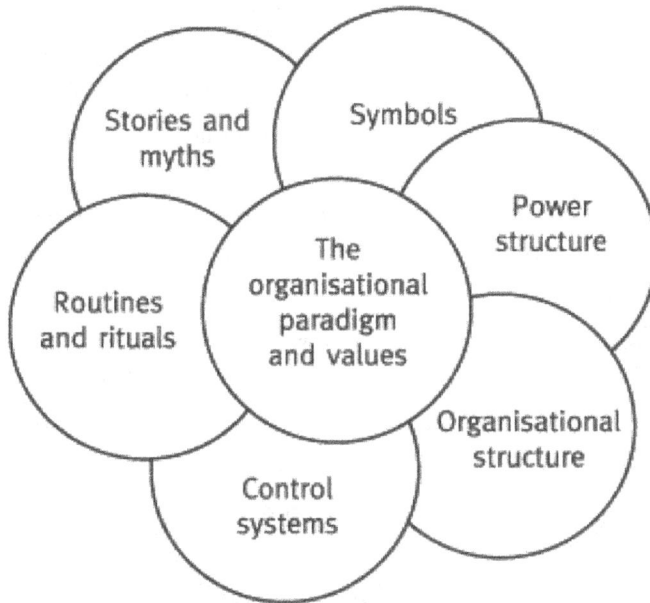

Figure 12: The Cultural Web

The cultural web above was devised by Gerry Johnson as part of his work to attempt to explain why firms often failed to adjust to environmental change as quickly as they needed to.

He concluded that firms developed a way of understanding their organization (called a paradigm) and found it difficult to think and act outside this paradigm if it were particularly strong.

The different elements of the cultural web

The cultural web is concerned with the manifestations of culture in an organization and has six inter-related elements.

- ❏ **Routines and rituals** - routines are 'the way things are done around here' and may even demonstrate a beneficial competency. They can be the written or unwritten rules of the game within the organization.

- ❏ **Stories and myths** - that employees tell one another and others about the organization, its history and personalities; used to communicate traditions, standards and role models.

- ❏ **Symbols** - such as logos, offices, cars, titles, type of language and terminology commonly used which become shorthand representations of the nature of the organization.

- ❏ **Power structure** - formal or informal power or influence by virtue of position, control of resources, who the person knows, or history. This may be based on management position and seniority but in some organizations power can be lodged with other levels or functions.

- ❏ **Organizational structure** - reflects the formal and informal roles, responsibilities, and relationships and ways in which the organization works. Structures are likely to reflect power.

- ❏ **Control systems** - the measurement and reward systems that emphasize what is important to monitor and to focus attention and activity upon.

Many organizations find that some elements of the cultural web are easier to change than others. For example, it may be easier to change the formal organizational structure than it is to change long established routines and habits.

Organizational culture and people change

Culture and people change in an organization refers to a shift in employees' values, norms, attitudes, beliefs, and behaviour. Changes in culture and people pertain to how employees think i.e. their changes in mind-set rather than technology, structure, or products.

People change pertains to just a few employees, such as when a handful of middle managers are sent to a training course to improve their leadership skills. Culture change on the other hand pertains to the organization as a whole, such as changing an organization from a bureaucratic structure to a more participatory environment which focuses on employees providing customer service and quality through teamwork and employee participation.

An organization's values – what it holds to be important – are reflected in its culture. A manager's role is to ensure that the appropriate values are promoted, creating a positive organizational culture. The result is a thriving work environment with happy, motivated, and productive employees.

If leaders want to take stock of their organizational culture, they should take the following steps:

a) Identify the values that currently exist.

b) Determine whether these values are the right ones for their organization.

c) Change the actions and behaviours by which these values are demonstrated.

If a leader doesn't like the values discovered in step two, he or she can for example, opt to take training courses to learn to improve their own leadership skills, therefore effectively determining how to modify their employees' actions and behaviours (step three). If a leader conversely finds that the organizational culture as a whole needs changing, a company may offer training programs to large blocks of employees on subjects such as teamwork, listening skills, and participative management.

A major approach to changing people and culture is through organizational development. Devoted to large-scale organizational change, organizational development (OD) focuses primarily on people processes as the target of change. Organizational development is grounded largely in psychology and other behavioural sciences, although more recently it has evolved into a broader approach encompassing such areas as organizational theory, strategy development, and social and technical change (Wendell, L.F., Cecil, H.B., Robert, A.Z. 1994).

Used to create long-term policies for ongoing change, this approach applies behavioural science knowledge to the planned development of organizational strategies. Its goal is to change people and the quality of their interpersonal relationships. The aims of organizational development are as follows:

❏ Encourage cooperation

❏ Eliminate conflict

- ☐   Increase motivation
- ☐   Improve problem solving
- ☐   Open lines of communication
- ☐   Develop mutual trust

Popular organizational development tools consist of consultants, surveys, group discussion, and training sessions. Here's a brief description of some of the more common techniques used at these meetings (Nelson and Quick, 2005).

- *Sensitivity training:* is a method of changing behaviour through unstructured group interaction.

- *Survey feedback:* is a technique for assessing attitudes, identifying discrepancies in them, and resolving the differences by using survey information in feedback groups.

- *Process consultation:* involves help given by an outside consultant to a manager in perceiving, understanding, and acting upon interpersonal processes.

- *Team building:* includes interaction among members of work teams to learn how each member thinks and works.

- *Intergroup development:* involves changing the attitudes, stereotypes, and perceptions that work groups have of each other.

So how do managers know whether OD is working effectively within their organizations? The primary evaluation of effectiveness uses goals established when OD efforts and strategies began. Based on this evaluation, a manager can identify programs, strategies, and change agents that need to be redirected or improved.

CHAPTER REVIEW

The biggest challenge in every change effort is the management of the dynamics or the subtleties. One of the important factors in any change effort that must be considered and emphasized in an organization is its organizational culture. Culture according to Kotter (1996) refers to norms of behaviour and shared values among a group of people. Norms are common or pervasive ways of acting that are found in a group and that persist because group members tend to behave in ways that teach these practices to new members, rewarding those who fit in and giving sanctions to those who do not. Shared values are important concerns and goals shared by most of the people in a group that tend to shape group behaviour and that often persist over time, even when group membership changes.

The cultural web designed by Gerry Johnson is concerned with the manifestations of culture in an organization and has six inter-related elements i.e. routines and rituals, stories and myths, symbols, power structure, organizational structure and control systems.

A major approach to changing people and culture is through organizational development. Devoted to large-scale organizational change, organizational development (OD) focuses primarily on people processes as the target of change.

CHAPTER 8

Initiation, Maintenance and Sustaining Change

Gayla Hodges (2007) opines that the ability to change is one of the biggest differences between organizations that thrive because they are continuously innovating and those that stagnate because they are stuck in the same old patterns. Organizations that change own the future.

Lisette (2009) says that change is an unavoidable element of all of our lives, and the ability to seize the opportunities it provides underpins the success of all organisations. It is not enough for employees to simply survive change; people need to flourish in an ever changing environment if they are to realise their potential and thus contribute to organisation success: this requires courageous leadership. This leadership must be underpinned by good strategies, techniques and approaches.

Change is a function of:

☐ dissatisfaction with the present
☐ a shared vision of the future
☐ some first practical steps

Each of these elements is key and needs to be fully leveraged to bring about change. Change leadership is about tirelessly working on each of these elements. Change leadership is also about ensuring all the people in the organisation understand change and its personal and organisational impact; and have the capabilities and confidence to flourish in the changing environment of our business today (Lisette, 2009).

Managing the strategic change process

Change Management is both a *Science* – an intellectual activity – exploring and an *Art* – getting the people side of things right through talk. Managers must possess skills and apply techniques for effective change if organizations are to benefit from any change initiative. They must also consider change from a systemic view point because once the change is introduced, it may cause the environment or social system to react in certain ways be they positive or negative. A change in the social system also impacts on an organization's strategies. There is therefore, a strong interrelation between an organization and its environment. The figure below illustrates that interconnectedness.

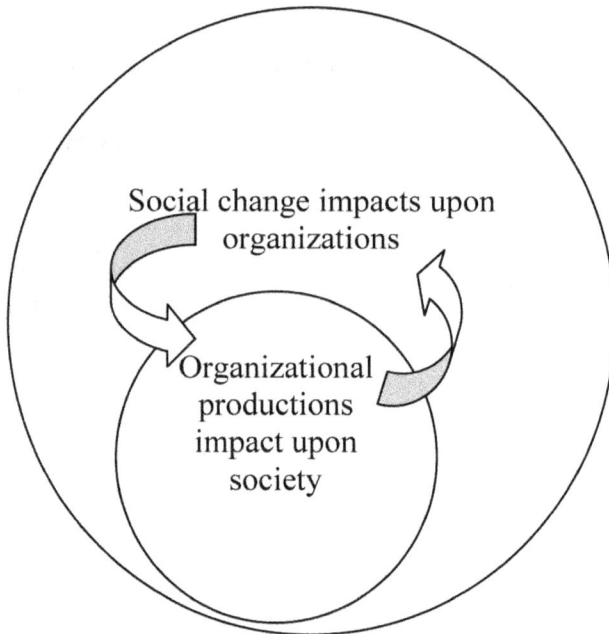

Social change impacts upon organizations

Organizational productions impact upon society

Figure 13: The interconnectedness of an organization with its environment

An agent of change - sometimes called the champion of change - can be defined as the person who seeks to initiate and manage a planned change process.

Davenport Thomes (1993) has identified several 'players' in the change process:

- ☐ The advocate, who proposes change.
- ☐ The sponsor, who legitimizes change.
- ☐ The targets, who are the people who undergo change.
- ☐ The change agents, who implement change.
- ☐ The process owner, who is typically the most senior target.

The change agent - is the individual or group who carries through change in an organization.

The implementation process involves three broad roles:

1. Change strategists – they are usually leaders who identify the need for change, create a vision of the outcome, decide what is feasible, choose who should sponsor and defend it.

2. Change implementers - make it happen by managing the day-to-day process of change; they must respond to the vision from above and the responses from below.

3. Change recipients - are the largest group including those who must adopt and adapt to the change; they are strongly affected by the change and determine whether it will hold.

The role of leadership is to anticipate the need for change, create an atmosphere of acceptance of change and manage the stages of introduction and implementation.

Negative attitudes towards change can be due to the following:

- ◊ Lack of understanding of the need for change.
- ◊ Uncertainty of the effect that the change will have on their lives.
- ◊ Self interest - people may resist change because it could take away something they value.

Change and communication

Effective communication is important in managing change. Effective communication is a key tool for managers seeking to drive successful change. Organizations that can communicate effectively about change increase the chances that the changes they undertake will be successful, and that the environmental changes they encounter will be understood. Organizations that mismanage communication about change or simply ignore the need for it when change is necessary, help guarantee their own struggles and failure to change (Axley 1996, p. 194; Kotter 1995).

Senior, B. (2005) asserts that change management involves a range of possible goals and requires:

i. Building unique internal capabilities. For a change initiative to achieve the desired results, the organization must build required competences and acquire the needed resources.

ii. Building fluidity for the unknown future. Organizations that are not fast, fluid and flexible will find it difficult to survive the rigors of the 21st century where the environment is very dynamic. Leadership is required to eliminate all forms of 'silos' such as time, location or operational. It must create a fast, fluid and flexible environment.

iii. Structural, cultural and system changes. All change initiatives, be they structural or system will have an impact on people. Leadership must build a culture that is adaptive and flexible. One whose people are open to new ideas and are able to identify new opportunities even during the times of great corporate success.

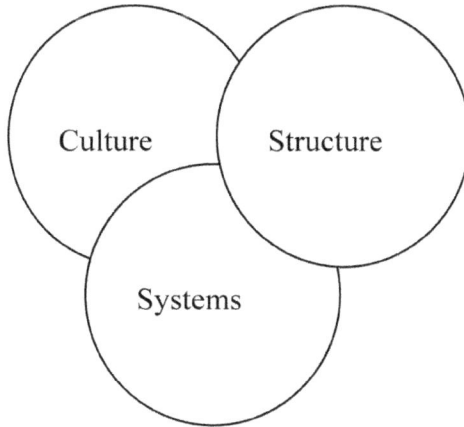

Figure 14: The interrelationship between organizational culture, structure and systems

The interrelationship between these three elements is critical if change initiatives are to achieve the desired results. Change is inevitable, fundamental, constant, essential, crucial, and continuous and as such, leaders cannot wish it away.

Change is about helping an organization develop adapting mechanisms in order to survive and to grow. It will call for continuous adjusting as a key to survival. Leading change successfully will help an organization to foresee opportunities, threats and challenges and to build competences to face and respond to these appropriately.

Leadership plays a fundamental role in change because it stimulates those involved in the change process by encouraging them to see the value or benefits of change. It helps them identify the need for change and motivates a person to stay calm in the midst of the shaking that is created by change. Leadership must help everyone see that the ultimate goal of change is the greater good for both the organization and its members.

Change initiatives will only succeed when an organization embarks on joint analysis or diagnosis of the situation. People must think critically and carefully as a team in order to identify the root causes or the driving forces of change. This will involve considering external and internal environments and appreciating that there is no one best way of managing change. Leadership must never ignore the forces of change both those for or against change. This will help the organization craft appropriate strategies to manage the change. Leading, controlling and managing the process of change are also important principles to be applied in leading change.

As mentioned in chapter four, several scholars and researchers have proposed various models of change.

Beer, M., Elsenstat, R. A., and Spector, B. (1990) advocate for a six step process as shown below.

1. Mobilize commitment through joint diagnosis
2. Develop a shared vision of competitiveness
3. Foster consensus for the new vision
4. Spread revitalization without pushing from the top
5. Institutionalize revitalization through:
   i. Formal policies
   ii. Systems, and
   iii. Structures
6. Monitor strategies and adjust in response to problems

Kurt Lewin saw change initiatives going through three major steps in the process of change.

☐ Unfreezing- identify driving and restraining forces
☐ Movement- initiate the change needed
☐ Refreezing- consolidate/anchor the change

John Kotter (1995) advocates for an eight step process:

1. Establish a sense of urgency by creating a compelling reason why change is needed.
2. Form a coalition with enough power to lead the change.
3. Create a new vision to direct the change and strategies for achieving the vision.
4. Communicate the vision throughout the organization.

5. Empower others to act on the vision by removing barriers to change and encouraging risk taking and creative problem solving.

6. Plan for, create and reward short term wins that move the organization toward the vision.

7. Consolidate improvements, reassess changes and make necessary adjustments in the new programs.

8. Reinforce the changes by demonstrating the relationship between new behaviours and organizational success.

Kotter's 8-Step Change Model

We look at Kotter's eight steps for leading change in detail below.

Figure 15: Kotter's eight steps for leading change

Step One: Create Urgency

For change to happen, it helps if the whole organization really wants it. Develop a sense of urgency around the need for change. This may help you spark the initial motivation to get things moving. Creating a sense of urgency is not simply a matter of showing people poor sales statistics or talking about increased competition. It is important to open an honest and convincing dialogue about what's happening in the marketplace and with your competition. If many people start talking about the change you propose, the urgency can build and feed on itself.

As a leader one can:

*   Identify potential threats, and develop scenarios showing what could happen in the future.
*   Examine opportunities that should be, or could be, exploited.
*   Start honest discussions, and give dynamic and convincing reasons to get people talking and thinking.
*   Request support from customers, outside stakeholders and industry people to strengthen your argument.

Kotter suggests that for change to be successful, 75% of a company's management needs to "buy into" the change. In other words, you have to really work hard on Step One, and spend significant time and energy building urgency, before moving onto the next steps. Don't panic and jump in too fast because you don't want to risk further short-term losses − if you act without proper preparation, you could be in for a very bumpy ride.

Step Two: Form a Powerful Coalition

In other words, convince people that change is necessary. This often takes strong leadership and visible support from key people within the organization. Managing change isn't enough − you have to lead it.

You can find effective change leaders throughout your organization and they don't necessarily have to follow the traditional company hierarchy. To lead change, you need to bring together a coalition, or team, of influential people whose power comes from a variety of sources, including job title, status, expertise, and political importance.

Once formed, your "change coalition" needs to work as a team, continuing to build urgency and momentum around the need for change.

As a leader one can:

- Identify the true leaders in their organization.
- Ask for an emotional commitment from these key people.
- Work on team building within the change coalition.
- Check the team for weak areas, and ensure that you have a good mix of people from different departments and different levels within the organization.

Step Three: Create a Vision for Change

When a leader first starts thinking about change, there will probably be many great ideas and solutions floating around. It is important therefore to link these concepts to an overall vision that people can grasp easily and remember.

A clear vision can help everyone understand why you are asking them to do something. When people see for themselves what you're trying to achieve, then the directives they're given tend to make more sense.

As a leader one can:

- Determine the values that are central to the change.
- Develop a short summary (one or two sentences) that captures what you "see" as the future of your organization.
- Create a strategy to execute that vision.
- Ensure that your change coalition can describe the vision in five minutes or less.
- Practice your "vision speech" often.

Step Four: Communicate the Vision

As a leader, what you do with your vision after you create it will determine your success. Your message will probably have strong competition from other day-to-day communications within the company, so you need to communicate it frequently and powerfully, and embed it within everything that you do.

Don't just call special meetings to communicate your vision. Instead, talk about it every chance you get. Use the vision daily to make decisions and solve problems. When you keep it fresh on everyone's minds, they'll remember it and respond to it.

It's also important to "walk the talk." What you do is far more important – and believable – than what you say. Demonstrate the kind of behaviour that you want from others.

As a leader one can:

- Talk often about your change vision.
- Openly and honestly address peoples' concerns and anxieties.
- Apply your vision to all aspects of operations – from training to performance reviews. Tie everything back to the vision.
- Lead by example.

Step Five: Remove Obstacles

Kotter opines that once you have followed step one to four and reached this point in the change process, hopefully, your staff wants to get busy and achieve the benefits that you've been promoting. The question however becomes whether anyone is resisting the change? And whether there are processes or structures that are getting in its way?

The thing to do as leader is to put in place the structure for change, and continually check for barriers to it. Removing obstacles can empower the people you need to execute your vision, and it can help the change move forward.

As a leader one can:

- Identify, or hire, change leaders whose main roles are to deliver the change.
- Look at your organizational structure, job descriptions, and performance and compensation systems to ensure they're in line with your vision.
- Recognize and reward people for making change happen.

- Identify people who are resisting the change, and help them see what's needed.
- Take action to quickly remove barriers (human or otherwise).

Step Six: Create Short-term Wins

Nothing motivates more than success. Give your company a taste of victory early in the change process. Within a short time frame (this could be a month or a year, depending on the type of change), you'll want to have results that your staff can see. Without this, critics and negative thinkers might hurt your progress.

Create short-term targets – not just one long-term goal. You want each smaller target to be achievable, with little room for failure. Your change team may have to work very hard to come up with these targets, but each "win" that you produce can further motivate the entire staff.

As a leader one can:

- Look for sure-fire projects that you can implement without help from any strong critics of the change.
- Don't choose early targets that are expensive. You want to be able to justify the investment in each project.
- Thoroughly analyze the potential pros and cons of your targets. If you don't succeed with an early goal, it can hurt your entire change initiative.
- Reward the people who help you meet the targets.

Step Seven: Build on the Change

Kotter argues that many change projects fail because victory is declared too early. Real change runs deep. Quick wins are only the beginning of what needs to be done to achieve long-term change.

Launching one new product using a new system is great. But if you can launch 10 products, that means the new system is working. To reach that 10th success, you need to keep looking for improvements.

Each success provides an opportunity to build on what went right and identify what you can improve.

As a leader one can:

- After every win, analyze what went right and what needs improving.
- Set goals to continue building on the momentum you've achieved.
- Learn about *kaizen*, the idea of continuous improvement.
- Keep ideas fresh by bringing in new change agents and leaders for your change coalition.

Step Eight: Anchor the Changes in Corporate Culture

Finally, to make any change stick, it should become part of the core of the organization. An organization's corporate culture often determines what gets done, so the values behind the leader's vision must show in the day-to-day work. The leader is urged to make continuous efforts to ensure that the change is seen in every aspect of the organization. This will help give that change a solid place in the organization's culture. It is also important that all of the company's management continue to support the change. This includes existing staff and new leaders who are brought in. If you lose the support of these people, you might end up back where you started.

As a leader one can:

- Talk about progress every chance you get. Tell success stories about the change process, and repeat other stories that you hear.
- Include the change ideals and values when hiring and training new staff.
- Publicly recognize key members of your original change coalition, and make sure the rest of the staff – new and old – remembers their contributions.
- Create plans to replace key leaders of change as they move on. This will help ensure that their legacy is not lost or forgotten.

Whatever model a change team settles for, it must ensure that proper diagnosis has been done, the right structures, systems and processes are in place and people are equipped to lead the change. Once the change initiative is completed, it must be anchored in the corporate culture for it to be sustained over the long haul.

The model below provides a generic approach to all change initiatives. Regardless of what model you use in leading change, it will have to contain the elements given here below.

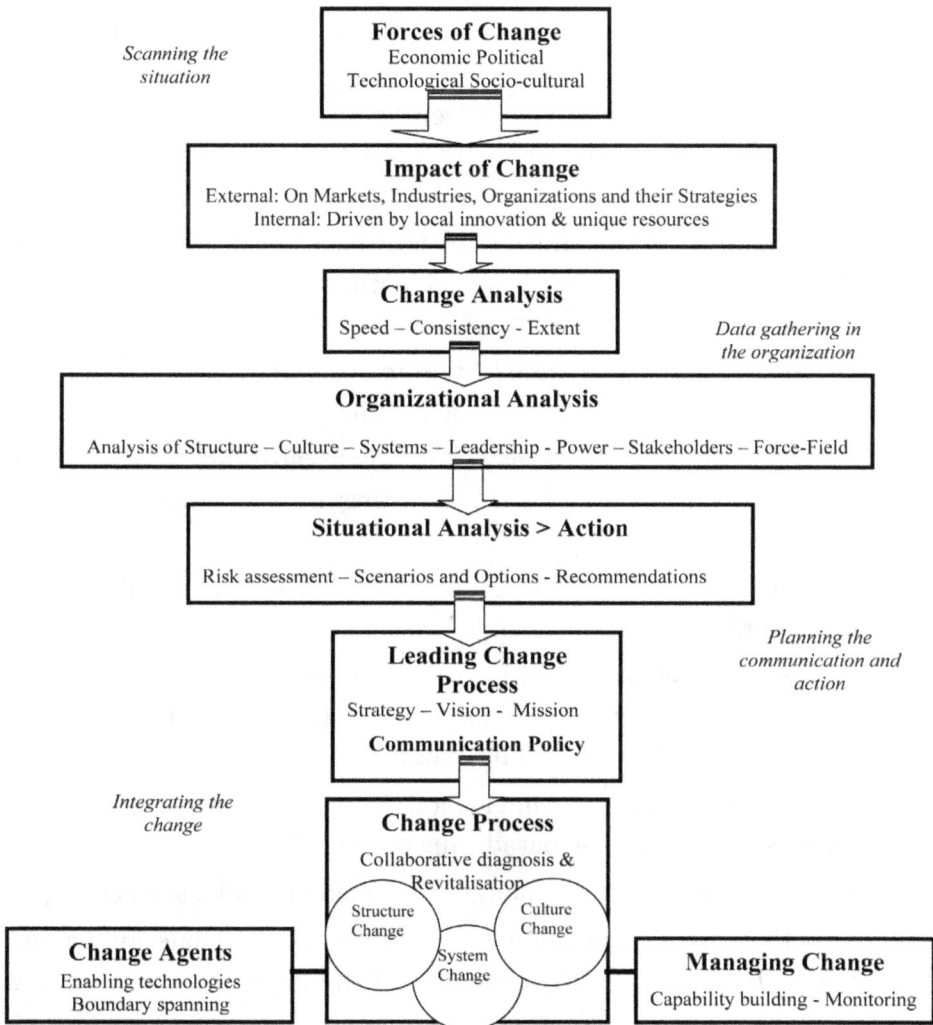

Figure 16: Model of managing change in organizations

Practical aspects of change in organizations

The following lessons must be understood by every team that is leading a change initiative.

1. The forces producing change may be socio-cultural, economic, technological, political, legislative or environmental in nature.

2. Change disrupts the markets relations of competitors, suppliers and customers, dislocating the existing product relations.

3. Change can be analyzed in terms of speed, impact, control and predictability.

4. Change may be externally driven by social and market needs or internally resource driven to improve the company or change society.

5. Organizations are open systems that have specific characteristics that make them different from each other in structure, culture and systems.

6. Organizations are mediated by external forces, internal cultural shifts, and by the passage of social time.

7. Change in organizations may be to create capability to drive social change, to react to social change, or to generate fluidity to prepare for future change.

8. Strategy and change management are inextricably linked, each feeding the other.

9. Organizations can be 'read' from their formal systems and from their informal shadow systems to understand their cultural, structural and system rigidity and fluidity.

10. Organizations can be understood from functional, interpretive, discursive and psychic paradigms or perspectives.

11. Leading and managing change is both an art and a science.

12. Effective change management is about the rationale for changing, the direction of the change, and the implementation of that strategy.

13. Organizational change should be framed to drive current company strategy, and to be strategic, by reshaping operational capability and flexibility for future organizational strategies.

14. Mapping stakeholders indicates the risk involved in changing by accounting for the likely impact on different groups.

15. Mapping the organizational force-field reveals the forces for and against change.

16. The force-field indicates the political landscape of allies, resistance and conflict.

17. Mapping the leadership situation indicates the style and capability that is appropriate for the context and for the leader.

18. Change management actions span a continuum between hard and soft responses to meet concrete or messy problems.

19. Change proposals are context dependent and contingent upon the situation, the time and the people involved.

20. Change management involves working with the existing discourses around and within an organization.

21. Change recommendations may include structural, cultural or system change strategies so that organizational form, behaviours and processes, are better aligned with company goals.

22. Structural change may impact upon very different organizational structures such as bureaucracies, project-based, matrix, vertical networks, and virtual organizational forms.

23. Cultural change is about reshaping assumptions, values and behaviours through framing the language and meaning within an organization, often for a new CEO.

24. Organizational learning produces conversations that build social capital, distribute knowledge and change systems.

25. System change may focus on customers, quality, re-engineering, benchmarking and performance monitoring to restructure the value chains for competitive advantage.

26. In knowledge work, the mining, acquisition, storage and distribution of 'lessons learned' becomes critical.

27. Leading change involves collaborative strategy formation and forming detailed communication policies.

28. Change processes must plan specific actions aimed at specific stakeholders.

29. Successful change processes include joint diagnosis, shared visions, consensus, revitalization, modelling, and the adaptation of structures, systems and policies.

30. Change processes need continual monitoring and adjustment.

31. Change 'agents' can model behaviours, span boundaries and lead enabling technologies to generate productive reflection and changed behaviours within organizations.

32. Managing change processes involves building capability, and improving competencies through workshops, coaching and mentoring.

33. Managing change involves monitoring change performance through benchmarking and balanced scorecards.

Strategies for change leadership

Effective change management occurs when the organization moves from its current state to a desired future state without excessive cost for the organization or its people. People resist change for a variety of reasons including inertia, poor timing, surprise, peer pressure, self interest, misunderstanding and different information (and aliments) of the change. Motivating people to change requires a general process of unfreezing, moving and refreezing with the caveat that appropriate and not appropriate behaviours be 'frozen'. More specific techniques to motivate people to change include education and communication, participation and involvement, facilitation and support, negotiation and rewards, manipulation and cooptation and coercion. Each approach has its, strengths, weaknesses and appropriate uses and multiple approaches can be used. More generally it is important to harmonize the multiple changes that are occurring throughout the organization.

A change may cause some loss to the person or organization affected by it. Attachments to old and familiar habits, places and people need to be given up. In major and unexpected changes, employees, groups and even divisions often experience daze, shock, recoil and turmoil. Some of the common sources of resistance to change include:

- ☐ Insecurity
- ☐ Resentment of control
- ☐ Inconvenience
- ☐ Threats to influence
- ☐ Economic losses
- ☐ Possible social loss
- ☐ Unanticipated repercussions

Transition Management

Transition management can be defined as the process of systematically planning, organizing, and implementing change. Once the transition from the old state to the desired state begins, the organization is in neither state, but in a vague state of transition. Transition management ensures that business goes on as usual under the old state, while the new state is being simultaneously implemented. Thus the two states tend to work side by side until the new state is a proven success, at which time the old state can be discontinued. Transition management is the responsibility of the normal management team, although an interim management structure may be created to ensure continuity and control during the transition period.

Dealing with individuals when managing change

Change is intrinsic to an organization and entails deviation from an organization's present form. To bring about organizational change through people is based on:

- What we understand about the nature of change
- The nature of human responses to change

The techniques and tools for managing the human and social aspects of change are less developed than the pace of change occurring in modern times. This deficiency can be overcome with:

- Enhanced motivation
- Commitment on the part of employees in handling the challenges of change

Dealing with individuals when managing change can be explained using the illustration below:

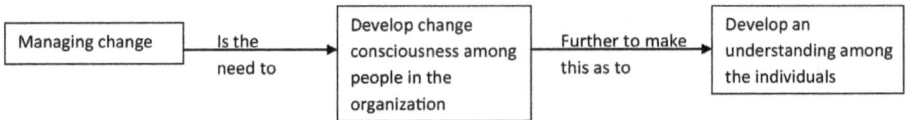

Figure 17: Dealing with individuals when managing change

Some of the ways a change leader can handle individuals when it comes to managing change and reducing resistance to this change would be to do the following.

1. Develop change – consciousness among people in the organization

Any organization in order to develop change consciousness has to:

i) Create a culture where employees seek change but are afraid to think and act differently to make change happen.

ii) Build a positive imagery for its employees of the envisaged changes to reflect a better future.

iii) Support the change process with adequate resources, processes and facilities.

2. Develop an understanding among individuals

The organizational leadership while initiating change has to examine:

☐ Change and employee attitudes
☐ Reasons for change resistance

- Personal loss (job security, salary and income, pride and satisfaction, job nature, friendship and associations, freedom to do the job the way one has been doing it)
- Negative attitudes
- Lack of involvement
- Personal criticism
- Loss of status and authority
- Inappropriate timing
- Cognitive rigidity
- Challenging authority

☐ Reasons why people accept change

☐ Assessing employee attitudes to change

☐ Dealing with individual resistance to change

☐ Individual – focused approaches to managing change and employee attitudes

Change and employee attitudes

The attitudinal continuum or reaction of an employee when presented with a change scenario can range from:

☑ Aggressive resistance

☑ Passive resistance

☑ Neutral

☑ Passive acceptance

☑ Active involvement

i) **Aggressive resistance:** May be exhibited in terms of:

- Complaints about and criticism of the change program
- Non-cooperation in change implementation or withdrawal

- Counter control activities
- Planned sabotage

ii) **Passive resistance:** Could be in the form of fake sympathy to the desired cause like:

- Spreading of rumours
- Reluctance to co-operate in change implementation
- Delaying change implementation

Dealing with this type of sabotage is difficult as it is usually the 'unseen enemy'.

iii) **Neutral:** Those who are related to the intended change may tilt either way positive or negative side depending upon what is advantageous to them.

iv) **Passive involvement:** Some employees are positive to the intended change (passive acceptance) more implicitly than explicitly. They recognize the need for change, but may not fully accept the way it is implemented, or else, they may work for it behind the scene. They are cautious and apply the watch and wait attitude towards the change.

v) **Active involvement:** is often seen in the words and actions of those who are highly positive about the intended change.

Resistance to change

Individuals resist change because it often requires them to think, feel and act differently from the accustomed regular ways. In addition, change may contract the mental maps they have in their mind regarding their work based on their experience and habits. Changing the mental map causes discomfort or pain. If the mental map and the change activity difference are minimal, the discomfort is less. Of course the reverse is also true. One's disposition also influences how one responds to change.

Individuals are characterized by different degrees of:

- Rigidity
- Emotionality
- Fear of failure
- Flexibility
- Suspicion
- Avoidance behaviours

Those predisposed to resist change

- Feel secure in being rule dependent and following the precedent or established procedures.
- Tend to be highly emotional, overexcited about change or become panicky and fearful. Over excitement may lead to emotional responses. The consequent negative outcome will result in an individual behaving in a defensive manner.
- Are overly suspicious; see all kinds of motives in others' behaviour.
- Are conscious of their failures rather than their successes and avoid anything that is different from the familiar and habitual.

Individual responses to change discussed below, are also influenced by their orientation to time as shown in figure 18.

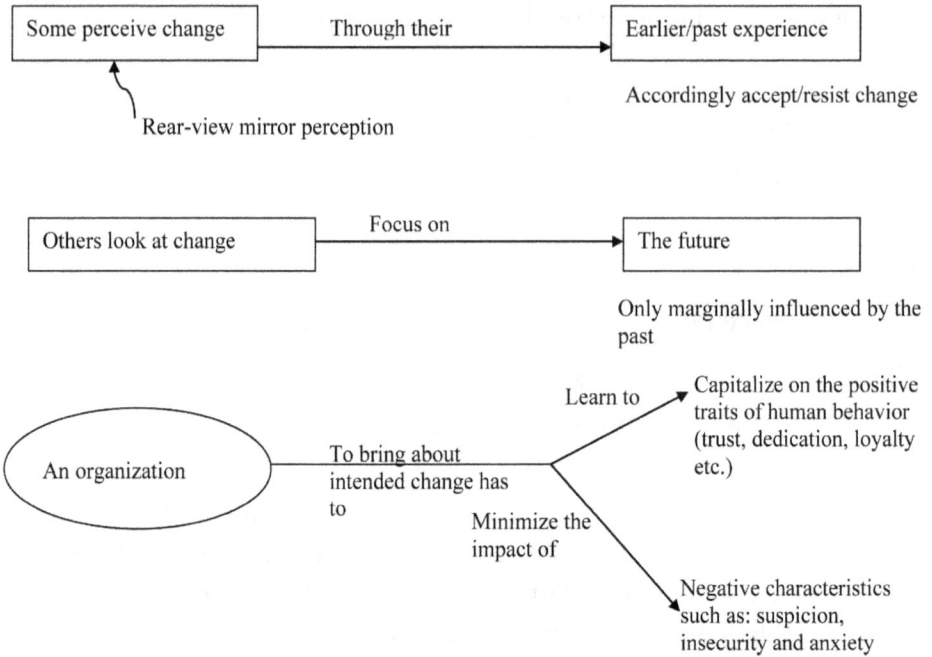

Figure 18: Individual Response to Change Activities in an Organization

Negative attitudes: People who resist change are usually those with negative attitudes towards their organization/superiors due to lack of trust, that might have resulted from a bitter experience.

Lack of involvement: Certain people who, are not involved in the change process and their ideas have not been sought for, resist change.

Personal criticism: Change may be considered a personal affront, questioning one's capabilities and performance and can be seen as a challenge to one's authority.

Loss of status and authority: Status and authority may be lost due to change to lower levels in the hierarchy (maybe loss of one's authority and power).

Inappropriate timing: When business is not good, change is introduced at that time. Everyone is fully engaged with more work to tide over the bad time. This may not be everyone's liking at that time.

Cognitive rigidity: Many people feel that old methods and old practices that have evolved over time may be the best. Some others see the need for change but are not convinced about the arguments in favor of change e.g. the unions of bank employees and associations to bank officers resisted for years the introduction of computers in banks of India. Their resistance was met with large monetary benefits to a limited introduction of computers in 1983.

Challenging authority: Some employees challenge authority to resist change.

Reasons why people accept change

The gains from change which people find in terms of values are:

* ✶   Security (about job)
* ✶   Monetary/other benefits (salary increase, more perks, improved working conditions, opportunities for developing more personal contacts)
* ✶   Status and authority (a new job title/office, special assignments)
* ✶   Personal satisfaction (arising out of an interesting job, more responsibility and authority)
* ✶   Job nature (challenging job, easier job)
* ✶   Opportunities to contribute to determine the change process

Dealing with individual resistance to change

Resistance to change is natural with individuals. They are to be motivated to accept change. Resistance can be considered as a function of one's attitude.

Though structures, systems and processes are needed, they are not enough to bring in change. These are, at best, either enable or perhaps may even be the blockers of change. It is the individuals who work on the above who can make change happen and achieve the highest levels of performance. Organizations should also link the creative and intellectual energies of individuals/teams/work groups with the change initiative and organizational architecture.

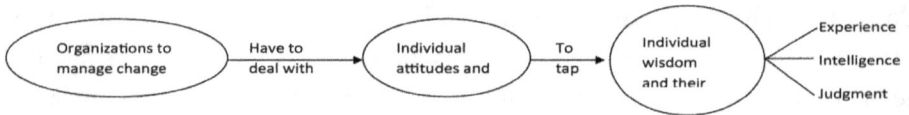

Figure 19: Approaches to Change Management

To motivate a person to accept change as well as to overcome their resistance, three dimensions are to be considered. Attitude is a system comprising of cognitive, affective and conative dimensions as discussed below.

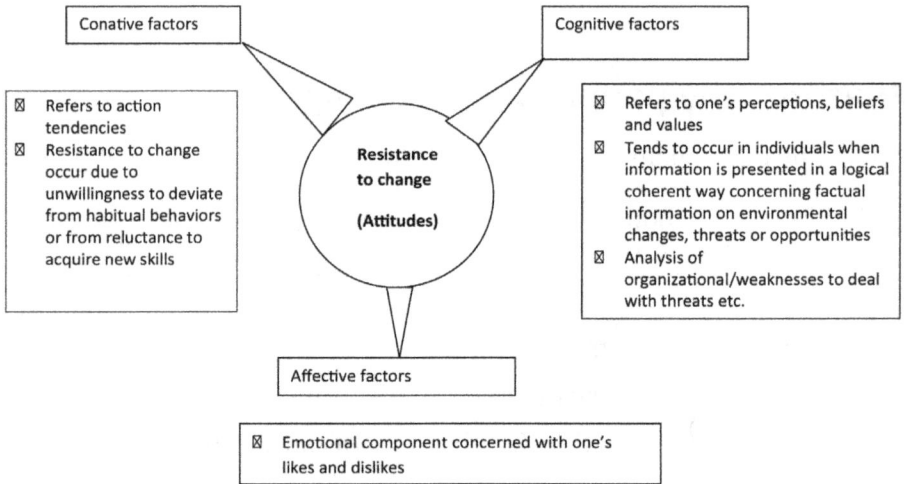

Figure 20: Factors for Resistance to Change

i.   The affective dimension

Change affects human emotions. Individuals fear and seek change. If an organization has to implement change, it has to anticipate individual's feelings about the intended change and deal with their emotions in positive and constructive ways.

Management can deal with change by:

- ❋   Creating feelings of psychological safety about the change, and about the desired state and the change process.
- ❋   Focusing on the benefits of change at the individual level.
- ❋   Demonstrating some of the benefits of change early in the change process.

The organization can induce positive emotions in their employees through:

- ◉ Employee empowerment
- ◉ Seeing employees as partners
- ◉ Compensation systems (includes different types of rewards) and dealing with negative emotions.

Some of the ways management can deal with negative emotions include:

- ✦ Empathy (putting oneself in the shoes of others and understanding their emotions and feelings)
- ✦ Mentoring (tutoring or counseling of an employee maybe by his superior)
- ✦ Manipulation (implicit attempt to influence others by the selective release or withholding information/incentives and the conscious structuring of events)
- ✦ Shock therapy (explicit coercion) putting people in a crisis or difficult situation
- ✦ Employee counseling

ii. The conative dimension

Conation means change can be facilitated in one's action tendencies. This is done by:

- → Clarifying contractual obligations
- → Emphasis on action learning implementation change
- → Cross-training (combination of information providing and skills practice)
- → Employee elasticity (stretching the potential)
- → Create the right supportive climate for optimizing employee performance through
  - • Organizational design
  - • Learning environment
  - • Information sharing

iii.   The cognative dimension

Change mechanisms here include:

- Explaining the nature and direction of change
- Communication
- Creating a common value orientation
- Employee training
- Participative management (employee participation)

Dealing with groups to manage change

A group can be defined as made up of people who are members of the same organization and occupy closely related positions in the organization.

Let us make a comparison of the dealing with individuals as compared to dealing with groups to manage change effectively.

Individual	Group

• Organization members have to deal with the cognitions, emotions and behaviours of each individual.
 	
• The dealing with individual attitudes is necessary; but may not be sufficient to bring about the desired support for change.
 	
• Individuals exchange ideas with others inside/outside the organizations to seek meaning, clarification and support regarding events and circumstance facing the organization.
 	
• An individual tries to seek support for his cognition in the beliefs, intentions and attitudes expressed by his/her peer group, the role-set members and other similar minded people in the organization
	• Group approaches to organizational change focus on groups as instruments of change planning and implementation and as facilitators or organizational and individual commitment to goals.
	
	• Group's attitude reinforces an employee's attitude sometimes.
	
	• The primary target of managing change would be:
	  – The group itself
	  – The relationship among its members
	
	• Forms of group based changes are:
	  – Sensitivity training
	  – Team building
	  – Self managed teams

Table 1: Differences between Individuals and Groups with regard to dealing with change

Group members often emerge with a restructuring of their values about people and their operations in group settings. Forms of group based changes include the following:

1. Sensitivity training

It was first used in Bethel, Maine in 1947. The technique is based on the use of peer groups for individual and organizational change.

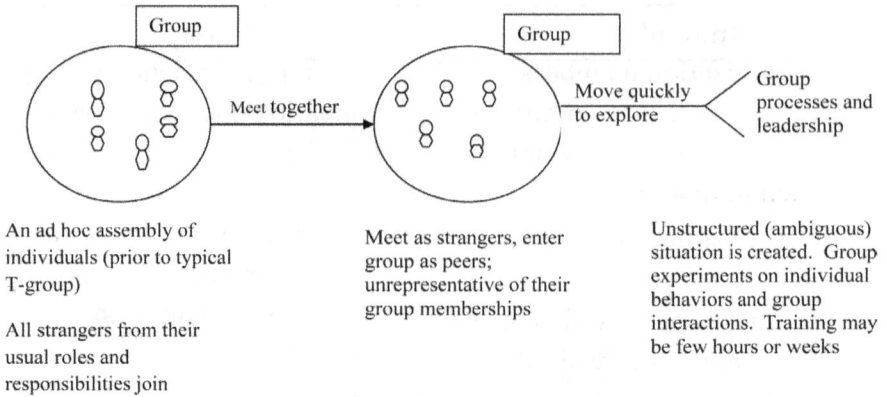

An ad hoc assembly of individuals (prior to typical T-group)

All strangers from their usual roles and responsibilities join

Meet as strangers, enter group as peers; unrepresentative of their group memberships

Unstructured (ambiguous) situation is created. Group experiments on individual behaviors and group interactions. Training may be few hours or weeks

Figure 21: Sensitivity Training

The trainer plays a passive role in the training process. The environment is helpful for anybody to talk freely on the subject. They can express views freely and not to be punished. Opportunities are provided to understand the behaviour of the individuals and that of others.

Stage 1 (Beginning)	Stage 2 (Mid period)	Stage 3 (End)
☒ Self contained series of events (periods of strangeness and uncertainty found) ⇒ ☒ Begins without an agenda, a structure, and division of labor or rules of procedure. ☒ People in each group are strangers to each other; brought to work on a common goal of learning more about themselves, the impact they have on others, to learn how groups can become effective instruments for meeting the needs of others.	Self discovery ⇒	Goal is to gain an insight into the groups development. Members of the group attain increased sensitivity to their own behaviour, the action of others, and to the nature of group development.

Table 2: Sensitivity training process

The intervention-through-sensitivity training is helpful in:

- Understanding one's own behaviour
- Understanding how one's behaviour affects other's behaviour
- Understanding why people behave the way they do
- Encouraging one to try out new ways of interacting with people and receiving feedback
- Understanding group processes

- Developing increased tolerance for other people's behaviour

2. Team building

A team can be defined as a group of individuals who tend to work independently to achieve organizational objectives and their own individual objectives. A team is characterized by:

- Working together for a reason
- Interdependency (skills, abilities of individuals are mutually supportive)
- Commitment to and belief in working together
- Accountability (for performance)

Team effort forms 90% of any organization's activity. It is important in an organization for the following purposes:

- To meet with the increasing environmental pressures on business
- To bring about changes in an organization

An effective team member should:

- Understand and be committed to group goals, and values his team membership
- Be friendly, concerned and interested in others
- Listen to others, and contributions of others
- Recognize and respect individual differences
- Include others in the decision making processes
- Acknowledge interpersonal conflicts and deal with them properly

How to build a team

The stages below can be used to build a team. In each stage, two basic orientations are to be built into the thinking and behaviours of the members:

- Orientation to goals and talks
- Orientation to people and relationships

Stage 1: Building awareness and forming the group (members are made to study the change initiative, change process, desired goals, tasks to be performed individually by members, the connectedness of tasks to the achievement of the goal, the identification of the individuals at every point). Identify the need for the change, how to bring about the change, by whom, in each of the change process to be properly identified.

Stage 2: Confrontation with issues, problems and conflicts (one of facing reality).

Stage 3: Maximizing cooperation (after individuals are clear about their roles and the interconnections).

Stage 4: Focused on change implementation/goal achievement/generation of ideas, problem solving and decision making.

Barriers to effective change

No matter how necessary change seems to upper management, many barriers must be broken down if a planned strategic change is to be implemented successfully. The key to successful change is in the planning and the implementation. A leader's job is to help reduce these barriers so as to effortlessly move the organization forward. The following are barriers to successful change implementation. In *Leading Change: A guide for managers*, the Robert Gordon University gives the following barriers to effective change implementation.

The compelling case for change

◊   Failing to "paint the right picture" of the future state

◊   Poor employee involvement and discussion

◊   Failing to build up the case for change over time – too rushed

◊   Failing to share key data with employees – lack of transparency

Not understanding what change is

◊ Failing to see change as a journey, not a single event

◊ Over-simplified view of "getting the change out the way"

Employee involvement

◊ When the planning team is too narrowly defined or too focused on objective analysis and critical thinking, it becomes too easy to lose sight of the fact that the planned change will affect people. When the feelings of employees are overlooked, the result is often deep resentment because some unrecognized taboo or tradition has not been duly respected.

◊ Failing to involve employee teams in optimizing solutions and developing implementation plans that will work!

◊ Successes are not recognised, communicated and/or celebrated

Ownership confusion

◊ Failing to establish clearly **who** is responsible for **what**, and **who** is making the decisions

◊ No engagement and/or buy-in of key stakeholders

Ineffective implementation

◊ Viewing implementation as the "easy part"!

◊ Failing to clarify who is coordinating implementation

◊ An unclear transition plan of roles and responsibilities

◊ Poor alignment of senior team around leadership behaviours

◊ Poor communication – confusion about what is happening, and when

Perpetuating "the way we do things here" too long

◊ Failing to see the impact of the wider sector or economic environment

◊ "Good times" may have masked some less than effective management practice!

CHAPTER REVIEW

Whatever model a change team settles for (whether Kotter's eight-step process, Lewin's change model or Beer's et al six-step process), it must ensure that proper diagnosis has been done, the right structures, systems and processes are in place and people are equipped to lead the change. Once the change initiative is completed, it must be anchored in the corporate culture for it to be sustained over the long haul.

Some of the lessons that must be understood by every team that is leading a change initiative include the following:

* The forces producing change may be socio-cultural, economic, technological, political, legislative or environmental in nature.

* Organizational change should be framed to drive current company strategy, and to be strategic, by reshaping operational capability and flexibility for future organizational strategies.

* Change management actions span a continuum between hard and soft responses to meet concrete or messy problems.

* Change recommendations may include structural, cultural or system change strategies so that organizational form, behaviours and processes, are better aligned with company goals.

* Structural change may impact upon very different organizational structures such as bureaucracies, project-based, matrix, vertical networks, and virtual organizational forms.

* Cultural change is about reshaping assumptions, values and behaviours through framing the language and meaning within an organization, often for a new CEO.

* Organizational learning produces conversations that build social capital, distribute knowledge and change systems.

* System change may focus on customers, quality, re-engineering, benchmarking and performance monitoring to restructure the value chains for competitive advantage.

* Leading change involves collaborative strategy formation and forming detailed communication policies.

- Successful change processes include joint diagnosis, shared visions, consensus, revitalization, modelling, and the adaptation of structures, systems and policies.

A leader designs his or her change effort, and then faces the toughest step: the inevitable opposition. History shows that workers have resisted some of the best-laid plans. A few may openly fight it. Many more may ignore or try to sabotage the leader's plan.

Here are some of the most common reasons employees resist change:

- Uncertainty and insecurity
- Reaction against the way change is presented
- Threats to vested interests
- Cynicism and lack of trust
- Perceptual differences and lack of understanding

To overcome resistance, leaders can involve workers in the change process by communicating openly about changes, providing advance notice of an upcoming change, exercising sensitivity to workers' concerns, and reassuring workers that change will not affect their security.

In addition, leaders are more likely to implement changes successfully if they avoid common pitfalls that cause changes to fail. Some of these pitfalls include:

- Inadequate change process
- Insufficient resources
- Lack of commitment to change
- Bad preparation
- Poor timing
- A culture resistant to change

CHAPTER 9

Strategic Thinking for Effective Change

According to the Government of Kenya (2007), Kenya Vision 2030 is the country's new development blueprint covering the period 2008 to 2030. It aims to transform Kenya into a newly industrialising, "middle-income country providing a high quality life to all its citizens by the year 2030". The Vision was developed through an all-inclusive and participatory stakeholder consultative process, involving Kenyans from all parts of the country. It also benefited from suggestions by some of the leading local and international experts on how the newly industrialising countries around the world have made the leap from poverty to widely-shared prosperity and equity. The Vision is based on three "pillars": the economic, the social and the political.

The economic pillar aims to improve the prosperity of all Kenyans through an economic development programme, covering all the regions of Kenya, and aiming to achieve an average Gross Domestic Product (GDP) growth rate of 10% per annum beginning in 2012. The social pillar seeks to build a just and cohesive society with social equity in a clean and secure environment. The political pillar aims to realise a democratic political system founded on issue-based politics that respects the rule of law, and protects the rights and freedoms of every individual in Kenyan society.

Strategic thinking is often described as reflective dialogue about the future so that one can avoid pitfalls as well as take advantage of opportunities. It is a process whereby you learn how to make your business vision a reality by developing your abilities in team work, problem solving, and critical thinking. Strategic thinking requires you to envision what you want your ideal outcome to be for your business and then works backwards by focusing on the story of *how* you will be able to reach your vision (Brice Alvord, 2008).

Put another way, strategic thinking is the ability to think systemically, with a whole systems perspective which often transcends what the organization is currently engaged in.

Strategy

Strategy is a term that comes from the Greek word, *strategia*, meaning *generalship*. Strategy is what you do and it is, in many respects, where you invest your funds and resources. A strategy is a long term plan of action designed to achieve a particular goal, most often "winning". Strategy is different from tactics or immediate actions. Strategies are intended to make the problem(s) easier to understand and solve (Alvord, 2008).

Strategy is about choice, which affects outcome. Many organizations survive – and do well – for periods of time in conditions of relative stability, low environmental turbulence and little competition for resources. Over time, virtually none of these conditions prevail in the modern world for great lengths of time for any organization thus the need for strategic management (Alvord, 2008).

According to Brice (2008) Strategic management is necessary in situations where an opponent blocks the way to an objective. Strategic thinking breaks the chains that currently anchor an individual or organization in survival mode. Strategic thinking requires that one take a critical look at the underlying factors that lead to successful strategic planning.

Strategy should be adaptable rather than a rigid set of instructions which is why strategic thinking is so important.

Goals

Creating a strategy for any organization involves defining goals and intermediate and short-term objectives. Your goals are the broad results you wish to achieve over the long term. Your objectives should flow naturally from your goals.

Goals and outputs should always be clear and "SMART"

- Specific
- Measurable
- Agreed –upon
- Realistic
- Time – specific

Additionally, as a leader you should:

- Ask yourself what things are important to the organization?
- Find out what perspectives your management team have toward organizational priorities, and more specifically, your work team.
- Find out which of your priorities or goals have the best chance to be viewed positively at any given moment.

It is critical to ask if the right thing is being done within the context of the organization's strategic direction (mandate, vision, mission, core values and goals and objectives (expectations).

Strategic Thinking

What is Strategic Thinking?

Strategic thinking can be defined as a mind-set, set of processes, and range of competencies whereby individuals understand the strategic direction in which their organization is headed, know the relevant and situational strengths, weaknesses, and constraints especially as they pertain to their particular function within the organization, and are constantly scanning the environment to identify opportunities and threats that should be pro-actively addressed. When important issues are identified, action is initiated often in conjunction with others from across the organization (Yousie, n.d.).

According to Curt Buchholtz of Rocky Mountain Nature Association strategic thinking allows preparation to seize opportunities. It is a continual process of considering where an organization is today, where its owners or leaders want it to be, what is needed to get there and where the needed resources may be to make the necessary steps. Strategic thinking also helps an organization weather the storms (e.g., transitions in leadership and staff, losses in funding, community controversies), because a plan of action is in place *before* the storms hit — an important factor in sustainability.

Strategic thinking focuses on finding and developing unique opportunities to created value by enabling a provocative and creative dialogue among people who can affect a company's direction. It is the input to strategic planning – good strategic thinking uncovers potential opportunities for creating value and challenges assumptions about a company's value proposition, so that when the plan is created, it targets these opportunities. Strategic thinking is a way of understanding the fundamental drivers of a business and rigorously (and playfully) challenging conventional thinking about them, in conversation with others (Bob Garratt, 2003).

Strategic thinking is also about synthesizing, about using your intuition and creativity to formulate a unique perspective or vision of where the organization should be heading. It is pretty much like viewing a movie – it allows you to see things from "higher up." Strategic thinking is an attempt to think through as many "results" that come from our actions.

Strategic thinking is an ongoing process rather than a one-time event. Strategic thinking is not always easy nor should it be as it involves synthesis, using intuition and creatively forming, a shared vision, of where the organization should be heading if it is to survive and prosper in the current and future market place.

Characteristics of Strategic Thinkers

Strategic thinkers plan for the future: Plans provide a map to the future. They keep everyone on track and prevent "management by the bright idea" where you implement every idea that seems good at the time without checking its alignment with organizational direction and goals. Time spent planning is time well spent and actually makes it possible to accomplish objectives more quickly. A well thought out plan will consider necessary resources and specify actions, timelines and responsibilities that clarify where the organization is headed as well as the responsibilities of each partner. Without a plan, an organization could get stuck in a crisis mode – responding to emergencies and deadlines. They might be doing more but not necessarily better (Yousie, n.d.).

Strategic thinkers ask questions and evaluate progress: Always questioning is an element of strategic leadership. Some of the questions strategic thinkers ask include:

- Are we going where we planned?
- Are we meeting our expectations?
- Do we need to make any changes or additions?
- Is this helping us accomplish our mission and goals, and reach our vision?
- How well are we working together?
- Are there changes or opportunities ahead for which we need to prepare?

Strategic thinkers focus on these kinds of questions at every meeting. This helps to create a culture whereby leaders continually measure progress against plans, make course corrections and look to the future for new opportunities. This environment of questioning and evaluating helps to nurture the relationship because progress and accomplishments are more immediately apparent to everyone and create opportunities for regular celebration (Buchholtz, n.d.).

Strategic thinking must take into account:

- ☐ *Competencies and skills:* What are the company's strengths? How can these be used to create a unique competitive advantage? What are the company's weaknesses that might leave it vulnerable?

- ☐ *Products and offerings:* What is the portfolio of offerings (product, service, price and image bundles) that the company provides to the market? What are the overlaps or white spaces among the offerings? What is the rationale or logic for these offerings? What makes them unique? What are the brands associated with these offerings? How do these brands fit with the company's image? With each other?

- ☐ *Environment and industry:* What is the overall economic context in which the company competes? What is the regulatory or governmental environment, and how does this impact the company? What is the structure of the industry? Where is this industry headed, and where do we want it to be? What is our position in the industry, and what do we want it to be? How does this industry connect with others, and what are the implications of that for our positioning?

- ☐ *Markets and customers:* Who are the target customers for the offerings? What are their needs? How is the company uniquely suited to meet these particular needs?

- ☐ *Competitors and substitutes:* What is the nature of competition in our industry? What other companies have offerings that could meet the same needs? What are their unique strengths and strategies? How are they similar to or different from us? How might they respond to our strategies? Are there companies not yet in the market who might choose to enter it? What are their strengths and strategies? What market conditions might lead to action on their part?

☐ *Suppliers and buyers:* What other companies do we need to work with in order to make and sell our offerings? What is their relative power compared with us? What are their strategies and strengths, and are these aligned with ours? What's in it for them?

Strategy as a Learning Process

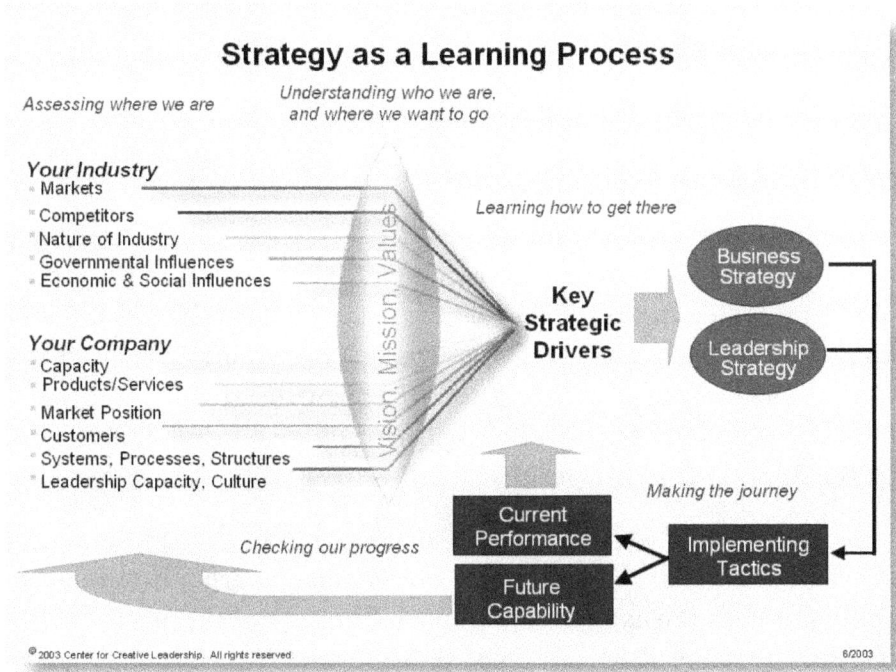

Figure 22: Strategy as a Learning Process

The Liedtka model of the elements of strategic thinking

Following the Mintzberg model, Liedtka (1998) developed a model which defines strategic thinking as a particular *way* of thinking, with very specific and clearly identifiable characteristics. The figure below illustrates the five elements of strategic thinking.

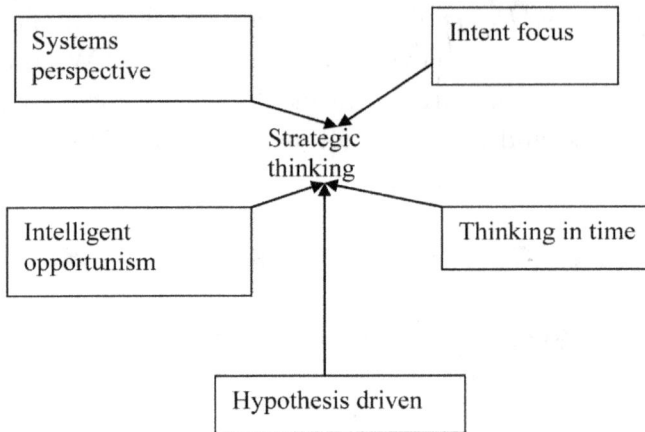

Figure 23: The Elements of Strategic Thinking

The first element is a *systems perspective.* A strategic thinker has a mental model of the complete system of value creation from beginning to end, and understands the interdependencies within the chain. Peter Senge (1990) also stresses the significance of mental models in influencing our behaviour. According to Peter, new insights fail to get put into practice because they conflict with deeply held internal images of how the world works, images that limit us to familiar ways of thinking and acting.

The mental model of how the world works must incorporate an understanding of both the external and internal context of the organization. According to James Moore (1993) these mental models must lead to the perception of a business in a context larger than that of the industry in order to facilitate innovation. As James puts it:

> I suggest that a company be viewed not as a member of a single industry but as part of a *business ecosystem* that crosses a variety of industries. In a business ecosystem, companies co-evolve capabilities around a new innovation: they work co-operatively and competitively to support new products, satisfy customer needs, and eventually incorporate the next round of innovations.

Thus the ability to manage in these converging arenas requires that leaders think strategically about the alliances they make within these competing networks and how they position themselves and their organizations within this ecosystem.

In addition to understanding the external business ecosystem in which a firm operates, strategic thinkers must also appreciate the inter-relationships among the individual internal parts that, together, constitute the whole, as well as the fact that the whole is greater than the sum of its parts.

Senge (1990) uses the term *systems thinking* to describe the sample phenomenon, and suggests that it is arguably the most critical of the five disciplines of the learning organization. He advocates that systems thinking is what makes all other types of learning work in harmony and points out that a fundamental problem for business organizations is the failure to see problems as elements of systems failures because *"most of an organization's problems are not unique errors but systems issues"*.

The systems perspective enables individuals to clarify their role within the larger system and the impact of their behaviour on other parts of the system, as well as on the final outcome. This approach addresses, therefore, not only the fit between the corporate, business, and functional levels of strategy, but very importantly, the person level. According to Liedtka (1998):

> It is impossible to optimize the outcome of the system for the end customer, without such understanding. The potential for damage wrought by well-intentioned but parochial managers optimizing their part of the system at the expense of the whole is substantial.

Thus, from a vertical perspective, strategic thinkers see the linkages in the system from multiple perspectives and understand the relationship among the corporate, business, and functional levels of strategies to the external context, as well as to the personal daily choices they make. From a horizontal perspective, they also understand the connections across departments and functions, and between suppliers and buyers.

The second element of strategic thinking is that it is ***intent-focused*** and intent-driven.

Strategic intent is a term that implies a particular point of view about the long-term market or competitive position that a firm hopes to build over the coming decade or so. Hence, it conveys *a sense of direction*. Strategic intent has an emotional edge to it; it is a goal that employees perceive as inherently worthwhile. Hence, it implies a *sense of destiny*. Direction, discovery, and destiny. These are the attributes of strategic intent.

Strategic intent provides the focus that allows individuals within an organization or marshal and leverage their energy, to focus attention, to resist distraction, and to concentrate for as long as it takes to achieve a goal (Hamel and Prahalad, 1994).

Therefore, strategic thinking is fundamentally concerned with, and driven by, the continuous shaping and re-shaping of intent.

The third element of strategic thinking is ***intelligent opportunism.*** The essence of this notion is the idea of openness to new experience which allows one to take advantage of alternative strategies that may emerge as more relevant to a rapidly changing business environment. Mintzberg (1999) sees this approach as underscoring the difference between *emergent strategy* and *deliberate strategy*.

In practicing intelligent opportunism, it is important that organizations seriously consider the input from lower level employees or more innovative employees who may be instrumental in embracing or identifying alterative strategies that may be more appropriate for the environment. For example, Intel's predominant role in the microprocessor industry was largely the result of a renegade band of scientists acting in defiance of senior management's stated strategic objectives. Given this, one can well imagine the loss to industry if the focus is only rigidly defined and mandated top-down strategies to the exclusion of other emerging strategies and voices of dissent!

The fourth element of strategic thinking is referred to as ***thinking in time.*** According to Hamel and Parhalad (1994), strategy is not solely driven by the future, but by the gap between the current reality and the intent for the future. According to them:

Strategic intent implies a sizeable stretch for an organization. Current capabilities and resources will not suffice. This forces the organization to be more inventive, to make the most of limited resources. Whereas the traditional view of strategy focuses on the degree of fit between existing resources and current opportunities, strategic intent creates an extreme misfit between resources and ambitions.

Thus, by connecting the past with the present and linking this to the future, strategic thinking is always "thinking in time".

In a nutshell, strategic thinking connects the past, present, and future and in this way uses both an institution's memory and its broad historical context as critical inputs into the creation of its future. This oscillation between the past, present, and future is essential for both strategy formulation and execution. Charles Handy (1994) feels we need both a sense of continuity with our past and a sense of direction for our future to maintain a feeling of control in the midst of change. From his perspective then, the real question is not what does the future we are trying to create look like, rather it is "having seen the future that we want to create, what must we keep from the past, lose from the past, and create in our present, to get there."

The fifth element of strategic thinking recognizes the process as one that is *hypothesis – driven*. Like the "scientific method" it embraces hypothesis generation and testing as core activities. According to Liedtka (1998) this approach is somewhat foreign to most managers:

Because strategic thinking is hypothesis – driven, it circumvents the analytical-intuitive dichotomy that has dominated much of the debate on the value of formal planning. Strategic thinking is both creative and critical, although accomplishing both types of thinking simultaneously is difficult, because of the requirement to suspend critical judgment in order to think more creatively.

Nonetheless, the scientific method is able to accommodate both creative and analytical thinking sequentially through its use of iterative cycles of hypothesis generating and testing. Hypothesis generation poses the creative question, "What if...?" Hypothesis testing follows up with the critical question, "If...then" and evaluates the data relevant to the analysis. Taken together and repeated longitudinally this process allows an organization to pose a variety of hypotheses, without sacrificing the ability to explore novel ideas and approaches. The effect is an organization that can transcend simplistic notions of cause and effect and pursue life-long learning.

CHAPTER REVIEW

Strategic thinking is often described as reflective dialogue about the future so that one can avoid pitfalls as well as take advantage of opportunities. It is a process whereby you learn how to make your business vision a reality by developing your abilities in team work, problem solving, and critical thinking. Strategic thinking requires you to envision what you want your ideal outcome to be for your business and then works backwards by focusing on the story of *how* you will be able to reach your vision.

Strategic thinking must take into account the organization's competencies and skills, their products and offerings, the environment and industry they work within, their customers and markets, their competitors and substitutes, and well as their suppliers and buyers if they are to create competitive advantage that is sustainable.

Liedtka (1998) developed a model which defines strategic thinking as a particular *way* of thinking, with very specific and clearly identifiable characteristics or elements which are systems perspective, intent focus, intelligent opportunism, thinking in time and hypothesis driven.

Whether you sit on a board of directors, are a senior leader within an organization, or the most junior employee in the department, the ability to think strategically is important. It ensures continued focus on relevant trends in both internal and external environments which is key to effective decision-making at a personal, team and organizational level.

CHAPTER 10

Issues in Strategic Change Leadership

Change Leadership in the 21st century

Paul Evans (2000) asserts that leading change is not simple; it is to be taken as a balancing act. There is an absolute need for leaders to accept the challenge of navigating between opposites.

If management is all about delivering on current needs, then, leadership is all about inventing the future.

Paradoxes of leadership

These are found as under:

i) To be able	to build a close relationship with one's staff	to keep the staff at a suitable distance
ii) To	be tolerant	know how you want things to function
	be a visionary be dynamic	keep one's feet on the ground be reflective
	be sure of yourself	be humble
iii) To keep	the goals of one's department in mind	at the same time be loyal to the whole firm be able to cut through
iv) To try to	win consensus	
v) To	freely express your view ; do a good job of planning your time; trust one's staff	be diplomatic; be flexible with your schedule; keep an eye on what is happening

Table 3: Paradoxes of Leadership

Challenges of organizational change

Planning and managing change, both cultural and technological, is one of the most challenging elements of a manager's job. Managers need to be aware that organizations change in a number of dimensions that often relate to one another (Flakke, 2008). These dimensions include:

☐ *Extent of planning:* Although experts differ about how much change can be planned, managers still need to take steps to set up conditions that permit and even encourage change to occur.

- [ ] *Degree of change:* Changes may be incremental (relatively small, involving fine-tuning processes and behaviours within just one system or level of the organization) or quantum (significant change altering how a company operates).

- [ ] *Degree of learning:* This dimension relates to the degree to which organizational members are actively involved in learning how to plan and implement change while helping solve the existing problem.

- [ ] *Target of change:* Organizational change programs can vary with respect to the hierarchal level or functional area of which the change is targeted. Some changes are designed to influence top management and assist them in becoming stronger leaders. Other change programs may involve basic learning, such as customer services techniques for lower level employees.

- [ ] *Organization's structure:* Is it very stiff and bureaucratic? Is there a need for emphasis on policies, procedures, and rules? Some organizations are very stiff and bureaucratic and may need to "loosen up". Other organizations may suffer from lack of organization structure. They may need to emphasize policies, procedures, and rules.

Diagnosing the need for change

To plan change, managers must predict and diagnose the need for change. An organizational development theory developed by Larry E. Greiner (1972) is helpful in change management. Greiner's model shows an organization as it evolves through the five stages of growth, and the end of each of these stages is marked by a crisis that calls for a change. The five stages of growth are discussed below:

1. *Creativity:* The founders of the organization dominate this stage, and the emphasis is on creating both a product and a market. But as the organization grows, management problems occur that cannot be handled through informal communication. The founders find themselves burdened with unwanted man-

agement responsibilities, and conflicts between the employees and management grow. It is at this point that the crisis of leadership occurs, and the first evolutionary period begins.

2. **Direction:** During this period, a strong manager, who is acceptable to the founder and who can pull the organization together, is appointed. During this phase the new manager and key staff take most of the responsibility for instituting direction, while lower level supervisors are treated more as functional specialists than autonomous decision-making managers. Lower level managers begin to demand more autonomy, and the next revolutionary period begins.

3. **Delegation:** This stage often poses problems for top managers who have been successful at being directive: They may find giving up responsibility difficult. Moreover, lower level managers generally are not accustomed to making decisions for themselves. As a result, numerous organizations flounder during this revolutionary period, adhering to centralized methods, while lower level employees grow disenchanted and leave the organization.

When an organization gets to the growth stage of delegation, it usually begins to develop a decentralized organization structure, which heightens motivation at the lower levels. Eventually, the next crisis begins to evolve as the top managers sense that they are losing control over a highly diversified operation. The crisis of control results in a return to centralization, which is now inappropriate and creates resentment and hostility among those who had been given freedom.

4. **Control:** This stage is characterized by the use of formal systems for achieving greater coordination, with top management as the watchdog. It results in the next revolutionary period, the crisis of red tape. This crisis most often occurs when the organization has become too large and complex, and is managed through formal programs and rigid systems. If the crisis of red tape is to be overcome, the organization must move to the next evolutionary phase.

5. **Collaboration:** The last of Greiner's phases emphasizes greater spontaneity in management action through teams and the skillful confrontation of interpersonal differences. Social control and self-discipline take over from formal action. Greiner's model shows uncertainty about what the next revolution of change will be, but anticipates that it will center on the psychological saturation of employees who grow emotionally and physically exhausted by the intensity of teamwork and the heavy pressure for innovative solutions.

To plan change, managers must predict and diagnose the need for change. Greiner's model of organizational growth and change can help managers understand how the need for change relates to their specific organizational environments and the need for timely interventions if change is to deliver intended results.

Steps in planned change

Once an organization's management commits to planned change, they need to create a logical step-by-step approach in order to accomplish the objectives (Kritsonis, 2005). Planned change requires managers to follow an eight-step process for successful implementation, which is illustrated in the figure below.

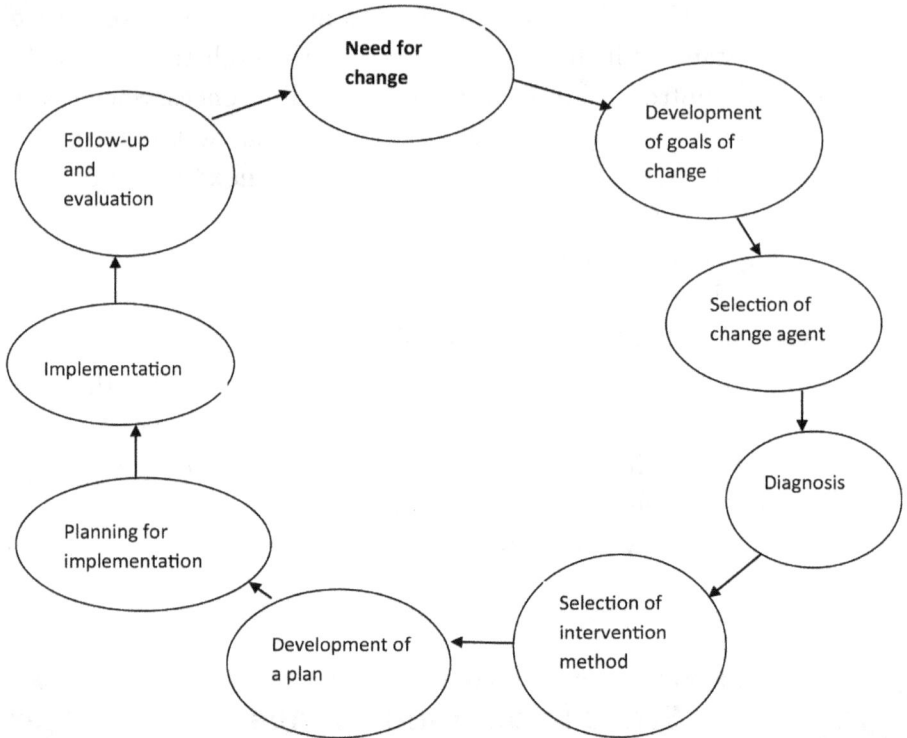

Figure 24: Steps in planned change

CHAPTER REVIEW

Planning and managing change, both cultural and technological, is one of the most challenging elements of a manager's job. Managers need to be aware that organizations change in the following dimensions that often relate to one another.

- Extent of planning
- Degree of change
- Degree of learning
- Target of change
- Organization's structure

To plan change, managers must predict and diagnose the need for change. Greiner's model shows an organization as it evolves through the five stages of growth, and the end of each of these stages is marked by a crisis that calls for a change. The five stages of growth are:

* Creativity
* Direction
* Delegation
* Control
* Collaboration

Once an organization's management commits to planned change, they need to create a logical step-by step approach in order to accomplish the objectives. Planned change requires leaders and managers to follow an eight-step process for successful implementation as follows:

Need for change

1. Development of goals of change
2. Selection of change agent
3. Diagnosis
4. Selection of intervention method
5. Development of a plan
6. Planning for implementation
7. Implementation
8. Follow-up and evaluation

CHAPTER 11

Building a Learning Organization

A learning organization is the term given to a company that facilitates the learning of its members and continuously transforms itself. Learning organizations develop as a result of the pressures facing modern organizations that enable them remain competitive in their business environment (Senge, 2002).

Peter Senge(2002), a business management guru defines learning organizations as "Organizations where people continually expand their capacity to create the results they truly desire, where new and expansive patterns of thinking are nurtured, where collective aspiration is set free, and where people are continually learning to learn together."

Organizations do not organically develop into learning organizations. There are factors prompting their change. As organizations grow, they lose their capacity to learn as company structures and individual thinking becomes rigid. When problems arise, the proposed solutions often turn out to be only short term (single loop learning) and re-emerge in the future. To remain competitive, many organizations have restructured, with fewer people in the company. This means those who remain need to work more effectively. To create a competitive advantage, companies need to learn faster than their competitors and to develop a customer responsive culture. Argyris, (1995) opined that organizations need to maintain knowledge about new products and processes, understand what is happening in the outside environment and produce creative solutions using the knowledge and skills of all within the organization. This requires co-operation between individuals and groups, free and reliable communication, and a culture of trust.

Benefits of maintaining a learning organization culture

The main benefits are;

- Maintaining levels of innovation and remaining competitive
- Being better placed to respond to external pressures
- Having the knowledge to better link resources to customer needs
- Improving quality of outputs at all levels
- Improving corporate image by becoming more people oriented
- Increasing the pace of change within the organization.

Characteristics of a learning organization

A learning organization exhibits five main characteristics: systems thinking, personal mastery, mental models, a shared vision, and team learning.

Systems' thinking: The idea of the learning organization developed from a body of work called systems' thinking. This is a conceptual framework that allows people to study businesses as bounded objects. Learning organizations use this method of thinking when assessing their company and have information systems that measure the performance of the organization as a whole and of its various components. Systems' thinking states that all the characteristics must be apparent at once in an organization for it to be a learning organization. If some of these characteristics are missing, then the organization will fall short of its goal. However O'Keeffe and Jančev, (2003) believe that the characteristics of a learning organization are factors that are gradually acquired, rather than developed simultaneously.

Personal mastery: The commitment by an individual to the process of learning is known as personal mastery. There is a competitive advantage for an organization whose workforce can learn quicker than the workforce of other organizations. Individual learning is acquired through staff training and development. However, learning cannot be forced upon an individual who is not receptive to learning. Research shows that most learning in the workplace is incidental, rather than the product of formal training therefore it is important to develop a culture where personal mastery is practiced in daily life. A learning organization has been described as the sum of individual learning, but there must be mechanisms for individual learning to be transferred into organizational learning.

Mental models: The assumptions held by individuals and organizations are called mental models. To become a learning organization, these models must be challenged. Individuals tend to espouse theories, which are what they intend to follow, and theories-in-use, which are what they actually do. Similarly, organizations tend to have 'memories' which preserve certain behaviours, norms and values. In creating a learning environment it is important to replace confrontational attitudes with an open culture that promotes inquiry and trust. To achieve this, the learning organization needs mechanisms for locating and assessing organizational theories of action. Unwanted values need to be discarded in a process called 'unlearning'. Wang and Ahmed (2002) refer to this as 'triple loop learning'.

Shared vision: The development of a shared vision is important in motivating the staff to learn, as it creates a common identity that provides focus and energy for learning. The most successful visions build on the individual visions of the employees at all levels of the learning organization, thus the creation of a shared vision can be hindered by traditional structures where the company vision is imposed from above. Therefore, learning organizations tend to have flat, decentralised organizational structures. The shared vision is often to succeed against a competitor, however Senge (2002) states that these are transitory goals and suggests that there should also be long term goals that are intrinsic within the company.

Team learning: The accumulation of individual learning constitutes team learning. The benefit of team or shared learning is that staff grow more quickly and the problem solving capacity of the organization is improved through better access to knowledge and expertise. Learning organizations have structures that facilitate team learning with features such as boundary crossing and openness. Team learning requires individuals to engage in dialogue and discussion; therefore team members must develop open communication, shared meaning, and shared understanding. Learning organizations typically have excellent knowledge management structures, allowing creation, acquisition, dissemination, and implementation of this knowledge in the organization.

The concept of continuous improvement

The concept of continuous improvement is based on the assumption that continuously striving to reach even higher standards in every part of the organization will provide a series of incremental gains that will provide a series of incremental performance. It consists of the organization creating an environment in which all employees can contribute to improving performance and overall effectiveness as a normal and continuing part of their job. In an environment dedicated to continuous learning, the prime objective of managers and team leaders is to bring new ideas and concepts from their staff. Their task is to create an environment in which new thinking is encouraged and welcomed.

Members of the organization are encouraged to suggest improvement. The organization has to find answers to questions about its strength and talents, its weaknesses and what sort of organization it wants to be. It also has to cultivate its 'negative capability' i.e. its capacity to learn from its past mistakes. Explicit steps are taken by learning organizations to learn from experience. They provide forums such as development centers, team meeting, 'away day' conferences and workshops to enable people to reflect on what they have learned and what they still need to learn. Such reflections provide a basis for formulating organizational and individual improvement plans.

Checklist for a progressive culture

1. Does culture of the organization support and encourage new thinking and the involvement of employees at all levels in problem-solving and seeking improvement?

2. Is capacity to involve people in seeking improvements and having new ideas accepted, recognized and rewarded appropriately?

3. Are people encouraged to challenge traditional ways of operating?

4. Are steps taken by the organization to ensure that the top management and employees at all levels have the 'space' and encouragement to reflect on their experiences and learn from them?

5. Are managers and individuals encouraged to identify their own learning needs and set learning goals for themselves?

6. Are managers and staff encouraged to see learning opportunities in their day- to-day work?

7. Are system efforts made by the organization and its managers to provide new experiences from which employees can learn?

8. Are people encouraged to learn from their mistakes as well as their successes?

Organizational dimensions fall into two types:

a) Structural and
b) Contextual

Structural dimensions

Structural dimensions provide labels to describe the internal characteristics of an organization. They create a basis for measuring and comparing organizations.

1.   *Formalization* pertains to the amount of written documentation in the organization. Documentation includes procedures, job descriptions, regulations, and policy manuals. These written documents describe behaviour and activities.

2.   *Specialization* is the degree to which organizational tasks are subdivided into separate jobs. If specialization is extensive, each employee performs only a narrow range of tasks. If specialization is low, employees perform a wide range of tasks in their jobs. Specialization is sometimes referred to as division of labour.

3.   *Hierarchy of authority* describes who reports to whom and the span of control for each manager. The hierarchy is related to span of control (the number of employees reporting to a supervisor). When spans of control are narrow, the hierarchy tends to be tall. When spans of control are wide, the hierarchy of authority will be shorter.

4.   *Centralization* refers to the hierarchy level that has authority to make a decision. When decision making is kept at the top level, the organization is centralized. When decisions are delegated to lower organizations levels, it is decentralized. Examples of organizational decisions that might be centralized or decentralized include purchasing equipment, establishing goals, choosing suppliers, setting prices, hiring employees, and deciding marketing territories.

5.   *Professionalism* is the level of formal education and training of employees. Professionalism is considered high when employees require long periods of training to hold jobs in the organization. Professionalism is generally measured as the average number of years of education of employees, which could be as high as ten years in medical practice and less than ten years in construction industry.

6.   *Personnel ratios* refer to the deployment of people in various functions and departments. Personnel ratios include the administrative ratio, the clerical ratio, the professional staff ratio, and

the ratio of indirect to direct labour employees in a classification by the total number of organizational employees.

Contextual dimensions

Contextual dimensions characterize the whole organization, including its size, technology, environment, and goals. They describe the organizational setting that influences and shapes the dimensions. Contextual dimensions can be confusing because they represent both the organization and the environment. Contextual dimensions can be envisioned as a set of overlapping elements that underlie an organization's structure and work processes. To understand and evaluate organizations, one must examine both structural and contextual dimensions.

1. **Size** can be measured for the organization as a whole or for specific components, such as a plant or division. Because organizations are social systems, size is typically measured by the number of employees. Other measures such as total sales or total assets also reflect magnitude, but they do not indicate the size of the human part of the system.

2. **Organizational technology** refers to the tools, techniques, and actions used to transform inputs into outputs. It concerns how the organization actually produces the products and services it provides for customers and includes such things as flexible manufacturing advanced information systems and the internet. An automobile assembly line, a college classroom, and an overnight package delivery system are technologies although they differ from one another.

3. **The environment** includes all elements outside the boundary of the organization. Key elements include the industry, government, customers, suppliers, and the financial community. The environmental elements that affect an organization the most are often other organizations.

4. **The organization's goals and strategy** define the purpose and competitive techniques that set it apart from other organizations. Goals are often written down as an enduring statement of company intent. A strategy is the plan of action that de-

scribes resource allocation and activities for dealing with the environment and for reaching the organization's goals. Goals and strategies define the scope of operations and the relationship with employees, customers and competitors.

5. **An organization's culture** is the underlying set of key values, beliefs, understandings, and norms shared by employees. Those underlying values and norms may pertain to ethical behaviour, commitment to employees, efficiency, or customer service, and they provide glue to hold organization members together. An organization's culture is unwritten but can be observed in its stories, slogans, ceremonies, dress, and office layout.

Performance and effectiveness outcomes

The whole point of understanding structural and contextual dimensions is to design the organization in such a way as to achieve high performance and effectiveness. Managers adjust structural and contextual dimensions to most efficiently and effectively transform inputs into outputs and provide value. **Efficiency** refers to the amount of resources used to achieve the organization's goals. It is based on the quantity of raw materials, money, and employees necessary to produce a given level of output. **Effectiveness** is a broader term, meaning the degree to which an organization achieve its goals (doing things right) (Martinez, 2001). To be effective, the organizations need clear, focused goals and appropriate strategies for achieving them. Many organizations are using new technology to improve efficiency and effectiveness. For example, the health care industry is striving to increase efficiency by using information technology to reduce paperwork and streamline procedures. Information technology also helps the staff locate information more quickly and reduce mistakes, leading to higher quality of care and better customer service (Mihaiu et al., 2010).

Organization configuration

Another important insight from organization design researchers is how organizations are configured – that is, what makes up an organization's parts and how do the various parts fit together.

Mintzberg's organization Types

One framework proposed by Henry Mintzberg suggests that every organization has four parts. These include the technical core, top management, technical support, and administrative support (Lunenburg, 2012).

1. *Technical Core.* The technical core are the people who do the basic work of the organization. This part actually produces the product and service outputs of the organization. This is where the primary transformation from inputs to output takes place. The technical core is the production department in a manufacturing firm, the teachers and classes in a university, and the medical activities in the hospital.

2. *Technical Support.* The technical support function helps the organization adapt to the environment. Technical support employees such as engineers, researchers, and information technology professionals scan the environment for problems, opportunities, and technological developments. Technical support is responsible for creating innovations in the technical core, helping the organization change and adapt.

3. *Administrative Support.* The administrative support function is responsible for the smooth operation and upkeep of the organization, including its physical and human elements. This includes human resource activities such as recruiting and hiring, establishing compensation and benefits, and employee training and development, as well as maintenance activities such as cleaning of buildings and service and repair of machines.

4. *Management.* Management is a distinct function, responsible for directing and coordinating other parts of the organization. Top management provides direction, planning, strategy, goals and policies for the entire organization or major divisions. Middle management is responsible for the implementation and coordination at the departmental level. In traditional organizations, middle managers are responsible for mediating between top management and the technical core, such as implementing rules and passing information up and down the hierarchy.

In real-life organizations, the four parts are interrelated and often serve more than one function. For example, managers coordinate and direct parts of the organization, but may also be involved in administrative and technical support.

Contemporary design ideas

Each of the forms outlined by Mintzberg can be found among today's organizations. To some extent, organizations are still imprinted with the hierarchical, bureaucratic, formalized approach that arose in the nineteenth century. Yet the challenges presented by today's dynamic environment require greater flexibility and adaptability for most organizations.

The environment for today's companies, however, is anything but stable. With the turbulence of recent years, managers can no longer maintain an illusion of order and predictability. The science of *chaos theory* suggests that the relationships in complex, adaptive systems –including organizations – are nonlinear and made up of numerous interconnections and divergent choices that create unintended effects and render the whole unpredictable. The world is full of uncertainty, characterized by surprise, rapid change and confusion.

Efficient Performance Versus The Learning Organization

The new mindset has spurred many organizations to shift from strict vertical hierarchies to flexible, decentralized structures that emphasize horizontal collaboration, widespread information sharing and adaptability. This shift can clearly be seen in the U.S. Army, once considered the ultimate example of rigid, top-down organization. Today's army is fighting a new kind of war that demands a new approach to how it trains, equips, and uses soldiers. Fighting a fluid, fast moving, and fast changing terrorist network means junior officers in the field who are experts on the local situation have a quick decisions, learn on the job and may sometimes depart from the Standard Army Procedures.

Although the stakes might not be as high, business and nonprofit organization today also need greater fluidity and adaptability. Many managers are redesigning their companies toward what is called the **learning organization**. The learning organization promotes communication and collaboration so that everyone is engaged in identifying and solving problems, enabling the organization to continuously experiment, improve, and increase its capacity.

CHAPTER REVIEW

David Garvin, a professor at the Harvard Business School has discussed extensively what constitutes organizational learning and provides a helpful summary for this chapter. He states that for an organization to be effective in today's dynamic environment, it should be skilled at creating, acquiring, interpreting, retaining and transferring knowledge and purposefully modifying its behaviour based on new knowledge and insights. He lists five main activities that promote learning:

1. Systematic problem solving. Organizations must cultivate the habit of relying on the scientific method rather than guesswork for identifying and solving problems. They need to insist on data rather than assumptions for making decisions.

2. Experimentation with new approaches. This involves searching for and testing of new knowledge. It can take two forms;

   a) Ongoing programmes which involves a continuing service of small experiments to improve quality yields, productivity and reduce cost. Leaders involved in learning and change may also visit other organizations to learn from them. Successful ongoing programmes require incentives for risk taking and skills to perform and evaluate experiments.

   b) System – wide changes introduced in a single unit of the organization for developing new organizational capabilities.

3. Learning from their experience and history. This is based on reflection and self analysis. Garvin quotes the famous philosopher George Santayana, who coined the phrase "those who cannot remember the part are condemned to repeat it". Failure is the best teacher if one is willing to learn from it. Garvin distinguishes between a productive failure and an unproductive success. An unproductive success occurs when something goes well and no one knows how or why. A productive failure is one that leads to insight, understanding and adds to the shared knowledge of the organization. Learning from failure requires tolerance and patience. Organizations must give up the common pre-occupation with allocation of blame for failures.

4. Learning from experiences and best practices of others. This includes benchmarking and learning from customers. It requires open, attentive learning. Organizations must be prepared to face criticisms. Customers can provide up-to-date information, competitive comparisons, insights into changing preferences and immediate feedback on products and services.

5. Transferring knowledge quickly and efficiently throughout the organization. Learning becomes truly organizational only when it is spread throughout the organization. Mechanisms that promote transfer of knowledge include written or oral and visual reports, site visits and tours, personal rotation programs, education and training programs and standardization programs. Knowledge is more likely to be transferred when there are right incentives in place. As Garvin observes," If you don't change the way people are motivated, it is very difficult to modify behaviour." He notes that most companies are reasonably skilled at creating and acquiring knowledge but are much weaker on interpreting, retaining and transferring knowledge as well as on changing their behaviour based on their knowledge.

CHAPTER 12

Organizational Development and Change

Organization development (OD) is a unique organizational improvement strategy that emerged in the late 1950s and early 1960s. It has evolved into an integrated framework of theories and practices capable of solving or helping to solve most of the important problems confronting the human side of organizations. Organization development is about people and organizations and people in organizations and how they function. Organization development is also about planned change i.e. getting individuals, teams and organizations to function better.

Underpinning OD practice is a set of values, assumptions and ethics that emphasize its humanistic orientation and its commitment to organizational effectiveness. In a survey of OD practitioners, Hurley et al (1992) found that values were clearly reflected in five main approaches they used in their work:

1. Empowering employees to act
2. Creating openness in communication
3. Facilitating ownership of the change process and its outcomes
4. The promotion of the culture of collaboration
5. The promotion of continuous learning

Organization Development as a Planned, Systematic Problem-Solving Process

According to Rush (1974,p.32), an organization development process is "A planned, managed, systematic process to change the culture, systems and behaviour of an organization, in order to improve the organization's effectiveness in solving its problems and achieving its objectives".

Organization development is a group of activities initiated in order to enhance the organization's productivity and the job satisfaction of its personnel. Depending on the values in the organization, more or less emphasis is put on productivity and the working environment.

The organization development process is issue-oriented, focusing on existing and anticipated organization problems. Process connotes a series of interacting functions aimed at a logical goal. Change lies at the heart of organization development and it has as its target the elements of growth, effectiveness and excellence, thus implying that the organization is an open system that is capable of improvement on individuals, groups and organization levels.

Planned change involves a series of reinforcing activities undertaken with purpose and intent rather than something that happens accidently. Planned change further invokes a decision about the direction a process should take and it implies some ability to predict the outcome of the process through implementation of strategies designed to accomplish the desired objectives (Lippit,G., Longseth, P. and Mossop, J, 1985).

Organization development is a managed process that embraces not only the fact that there are means to guide and control the process but also the implication that the process is someone's explicit responsibility. The process is not left to take care of itself. The elements of planned and managed process carry the idea that OD is a systematic process based on a coherent body of principles, conducted by design and carried out methodically. The term systematic suggests unity in that each element of the process depends for its effective functioning on every other element.

The field of OD has developed several interventions to systematically address problems and opportunities through effective participation and involvement of organizational members. The field has accumulated principles and practical knowledge to guide managers on how to bring about change.

Organization development interventions present valuable ideas for structuring activities in such a manner that individuals and groups can bring about improvements and enhance learning. French and Bell (1999) outline the design considerations that OD practitioners employ for structuring activities to maximize learning:

1. Include the people affected by the problem or the opportunity. If the goal is to improve relations between two separate work groups, have both work groups present.

2. Ensure that the activity is not only problem or opportunity oriented but also oriented to the problems and opportunities generated by the individuals facing the issue. People feel involved and interested when they have defined the issues. They are more likely to follow up with appropriate actions.

3. Set in motion processes to help people clarify the goals and ways to reach the goals. Do not assume that destination and pathways are clear to everyone. It would be highly de-motivating for people participating in a group process to not know what the group is working towards and how they can attain the goals.

4. Ensure that the expectations are realistic. Even if the tasks are hard, complicated and taxing, they should be attainable. After the experience, success or failure in accomplishing the goal should be examined for learning.

5. Involve both people strong on experience and those with good conceptual understanding to bring in multiple perspectives.

6. Shape the mood and climate in such a manner that individuals feel

set free rather than anxious or defensive.

7. Design the process in a manner that the participants learn both how to solve a particular problem and 'learn how to learn'.

8. Individuals should learn about both task and process. The task is what the group is working on while the process refers to how the group is working and what else is going on as participants work on the task, such as individual styles of interacting, behaving and so on.

9. Ensure that individuals are engaged as whole persons, not segmented persons. This means calling into play role demands, thoughts, beliefs, feelings and strivings.

OD practice as a guide to effective change

These guidelines help the OD practitioner to produce effective change. All organization development interventions have a goal- transforming a part, an aspect or the whole organization. The guidelines are given hereunder:

☐ Maximize diagnostic data - start with interventions that generate data needed to strengthen subsequent intervention decisions.

☐ Maximize effectiveness - this can be done by developing readiness, motivations, knowledge or skills required by other interventions

☐ Maximize efficiency - work out sequence of actions to conserve organizational resources such as time, energy and money.

☐ Maximize relevance - deal first with the most immediate problems and the ones that have an impact on organizational performance so that the motivation to continue the efforts is maintained.

☐ Maximize speed - the sequence should also help enhance the speed with which ultimate organizational improvement is attained.

☐ Minimize psychological and organizational strain - to maintain people's sense of competence and confidence and their commitment to organizational improvement, choose those interventions that are least likely to create dysfunctional effects such as anxiety, insecurity, distrust, unmet or under-met expectations and unanticipated and unwanted effects on organizational performance.

Outputs created by OD interventions

☑ **Feedback**. People learn new things about themselves, others, group processes or organizational dynamics – data that either they did not know or did not previously take active account of. Awareness of new information tends to lead to change if the feedback is not too threatening.

☑ **Awareness** of changing socio-cultural norms or dysfunctional current norms. People tend to modify their behaviour, attitudes and values when they become aware of changes in the norms influencing their behaviour. Awareness has potential to lead to change because individuals seek to adjust their behaviour according to new norms.

☑ **Increased interaction and communication**. When individuals and groups have an opportunity to communicate with people that they do not normally interact with, changes in attitude and behaviour can result.

☑ **Confrontation**. This refers to surfacing and examining differences in beliefs, feelings, attitudes, values or norms to remove obstacles to effective interaction. Confrontation is a process that seeks to discern real differences that get in the way.

☑ **Education and participation**. Development of knowledge, skills and attitudes and increasing the number of people involved in problem solving, goal setting and generating new ideas increases the quality and acceptance of decisions, increases job satisfactions and improves employee well being.

☑ **Increased accountability**. This results from activities that clarify people's responsibilities and that monitor performance related to those responsibilities.

☑ **Increased energy and optimism**. Activities that energize and motivate people through visions of new possibilities contribute to effective problem solving and learning.

Building change capability

Organizations face three major challenges:

*   Increased competition for organization's resources.
*   Organization competing in a world that is constantly changing.
*   Globalization, technological changes and anticipated events.

According to Nilakant and Ramnarayan, (2006), a well known model of change management viewed organizations as going through long periods of stability punctuated by short bursts of discontinuous change. According to this model, periods of stability are periods of convergence. During periods of convergence, organizations make only minor or incremental changes to their strategies, structures, people and process. These may include: refining policies, procedures and methods; creating specialized units and linking mechanisms to efficiency and quality; improving selection, training and appraisal procedures; promoting organization commitment among employees, clarifying roles, status, power and procedures, in the organization, expanding a sales territory or introducing new machinery.

Introducing and implementing changes during convergence involve the following activities; generation and objective examination of alternatives; creating acceptance of the need for change through education and communication; participation of those affected by the changes; providing time to learn new activities; establishing role models; rewarding positive successes; evaluation and refinement. These changes can be designed and introduced by middle and senior level managers. During convergent periods, an organization becomes more effective and efficient. As it grows and becomes successful, it also develops internal forces of stability. As the organization becomes more stable, it also becomes more impervious to change. Therefore, it requires a frame-breaking change or an upheaval to ensure that it is in time with environmental changes. Frame-breaking change usually involves the following: a new definition of company mission and core values, an alteration of the distribution of power, a modification in structure systems and procedures, a change in the way people work together in the organization and new executives brought in from outside the organization in key managerial positions. In any upheaval, all the features listed above take place simultaneously and rapidly.

In today's world, where organizations have relatively shorter periods of stability, there is need for organizations to have an in-built capacity for adapting to change. Knowledge creation and diffusion is one way of creating such capabilities in the organization. Leaders must pay great attention to learning mechanisms and how to retain what the organization has learnt. The mechanism must help the organization retain the learning and knowledge despite the turnover of its staff. The organization must store or embed the knowledge that it creates in its systems, structures, habits and processes.

Change managers build capabilities by setting challenging goals, creating ownership, structuring activities to facilitate reflection and learning, initiating processes to accelerate unlearning and learning and fostering a behavioural context that is positive and learning-oriented. The basic leadership task in building capability is to develop people's confidence by demonstrating faith in their capabilities. Effective leaders build capability by making people believe in their own abilities to achieve challenging goals.

Building change capability is a process that involves four elements:

- **First,** capability is built by individuals and groups. Organizations do not learn; people do. Leadership should create opportunities for individuals to come together, reflect and act in order to build capability.
- **Second,** individuals and groups build capability when they successfully execute challenging projects. In order to build capability, individuals need to undertake a task that is slightly beyond their present capability. Capability is built when they successfully complete the task and reflect on their success.
- **Third,** building capability involves paying simultaneous attention to both action and reflection. Individuals and groups need to act

in order to build capability. There may be successes or failures, but it is necessary to study why things succeed while others fail. Reflection or learning from experience is crucial for building capability.

- **Fourth,** leaders and organizations can help individuals and groups build capability by providing a context that aids action and reflection. Organizational contexts that promote a positive behavioural climate tend to encourage building of capability. Leaders must set a powerful vision to align the people in the organization and unleash a whole set of learning initiatives. The organization must also be characterized by challenges, support for initiatives, role models and ready outlets for innovative spirit. Processes must also be in place for people to gain the necessary knowledge and empower them to apply the skills learned. The change programme must also become a process of modernizing mindsets and of changing the way people are motivated.

CHAPTER REVIEW

Organization development (OD) is about people and organizations and people in organizations and how they function. Organization development is also about planned change i.e. getting individuals, teams and organizations to function better. In a survey of OD practitioners, Hurley et al (1992) found that values were clearly reflected in five main approaches they used in their work:

- Empowering employees to act
- Creating openness in communication
- Facilitating ownership of the change process and its outcomes
- The promotion of culture of collaboration
- The promotion of continuous learning

Outputs created by OD interventions include feedback, awareness of changing socio-cultural norms or dysfunctional current norms, increased interaction and communication, confrontation, education and participation, increased accountability and increased energy and optimism.

Change managers build capabilities by setting challenging goals, creating ownership, structuring activities to facilitate reflection and learning, initiating processes to accelerate unlearning and learning and fostering a behavioural context that is positive and learning-oriented.

References

Adair, J. (2004). *The John Adair Handbook of Management and Leadership*, Thomas, N (ed). London: Thorogood.

Ansoff, I.H. & McDonnell, E.J. (1990). *Implanting Strategic Management*, Englewood Cliffs, NJ: Prentice Hall.

Axley, S. R. (1996). *Communication at work: Management and the communication-intensive organization.* Westport, Conn: Quorum Books.

Barbara, S., Fleming, J.(2006). *Organizational Change.* Third Edition. England: Prentice Hall.

Buelens, M & Devons, G (2004). 'Art and Wisdom in Choosing Change Strategies: A Critical Reflection', in J. J. Boonstra (ed.), J. J. Boonstra (ed.), *Dynamics of Organizational Change and Learning.* Chichester: Wiley.

Burns B. (2004). *Managing Change.* Fourth Ed. England: Prentice Hall

Communication-Intensive Organization. Westport CT: Quorum Books.

Conner, D. (1992). *Managing at the Speed of Change.* New York: Villard Books.

Drucker, P.F. (1988). The Coming of the New Organization. *Harvard Business Review.*

Dunphy, D. & Stacy, D. (1993). The Strategic Management of Corporate Change. *Human Relations,* Vol 46, no.8, p.905-20.

French W.L. & Bell C.H (1999). *Organization Development: Behavioural Science Interventions for Organizational Improvement,* New Delhi: Practice Hall, pp 146-147.

Garry L. (1997).What makes authentic learning organization –An interview with David Garvin. *Harvard Management Update,* June, pp3-5.

Garvin, D.A. (1991). Building a Learning Organization. *Harvard Business Review,* November-December: pp78-91.

Gilley, J. W. & Maycunich, A. (2000). *Organizational Learning, Performance, and Change: An Introduction to Strategic Human Resource Development,* Cambridge, MA: Perseus Publishing.

Gilley, A (2005). *The Manager as Change Leader,* Westport, CT: Praeger.

Harvard Business School (2005a). *The Essentials of Managing Change and Transition,* Harvard Business School Press.

Harvard Business School (2005b). *Managing Change to Reduce Resistance,* Harvard Business School Press.

Hurley, R.F., Church, A.H., Burke, W.W. & Van Eynde, D.F., (1992). Tension, change and values in organization development. *Organization Development Practitioner,* 29, 1-5.

Ibid: pp. 5

Ibid; pp. 149-150

Ibid; pp. 147-148

Hughes, R.L., & Beatty, K.C. (2005). *Becoming a Strategic Leader.* San Francisco: Jossey-Bass.

Jick, T.D. & Peiperl, M.A. (2003). *Managing Change: Cases and Concepts.* New York: McGraw Hill.

Jones, P., Palmer, J., Osterweil, C. & Whitehead, D. (1996). *Delivering exceptional performance: aligning the potential of organizations, teams and individuals.* London: Pitman.

http://kfknowledgebank.kaplan.co.uk/KFKB/Wiki%20Pages/Managing%20strategic%20change.aspx

Kanter, R. M. (1984). *The Change Masters.* London: Allen and Unwin.

Kotter, J. P. (1995). *Leading Change: Why Transformation Efforts Fail.* Boston: Harvard Business School Press.

Lippit, G., Langseth, P., & Mossop, J. (1985). *Implementing Organizational Change.* California: Jossey-Bass.

Lombardo, M & Eichinger, R (2000).High potentials as high learners. *Human resource management,* 39(4):pp 321-329.

Nadler, D.A & Tushman, M.L (1990).Beyond the charismatic leader: Leadership and organizational change. *California Management Review,* 32(2): pp77-97.

Nerson & Quick (2005). *Managing Change.* South Western: Thomson Learning.

Nikalant, V. Ramnarayan, S. (1998). *Managing Organizational Change.* New Delhi: Response Books.

Nikalant,V. Ramnarayan, S. (2006). *Change Management: Altering Mindset in a Global Context.* New Delhi: Sage Publication.

Rush, H.M.P. (1974). Organization Development in Practice: A Comparison of O.D. and Non-O.D. Companies. *Organization Development: A Reconnaissance,* 605, 31-33.

Schein, E.H.(1998). Coming to a New Awareness of organizational Culture, *Sloan Management Review,* vol.25, no1, p.94.

Senge, P. M. (2006). *The Fifth Discipline: The Art & Practice of The Learning Organization.* New York: Doubleday.

Senior, B. (2005). *Organizational Change*. Sydney: Pearson Educational.

Stickland, F. (1998). *The Dynamics of Change: Insights into Organizational Transition from the Natural World*. London: Routledge

Wendell, L.F., Cecil H. Bell Jr. & Robert, A.Z. (1994). *Organization Development and Transformation: Managing Effective Change*. Irwin: McGraw-Hill.

Wiliams, M.R. (2005). *Leadership for Leaders*. London: Thorogood.

Williams, M.R. (1998). *Mastering Leadership: Key Techniques for Managing and Leading a Winning Team*. London: Thorogood.

Williams, M. J. (1997). Agility in learning: An essential for evolving organizations and people. *Harvard Management Update*. May 1997; pp 3-5.

About the authors

KIRIMI BARINE

Dr. Kirimi Barine is the Global Publishing Development Consultant with the Global Bible Publishing unit of the United Bible Societies.

Barine is a founding Director of Publishing Institute of Africa and formerly the Publisher and Chief Executive Officer of Evangel Publishing House.

Barine holds a Doctor of Philosophy (PhD) from the University of Central Nicaragua and a Doctorate in Business Administration (DBA) from SMC University. His Dissertation was in the area of Governance and Leadership. He holds a Masters degree in Business Administration (MBA) and a Bachelor of Education degree from Kenyatta and Egerton Universities respectively. His research, teaching and consulting mainly focuses on Leadership, Governance, Organizational Behaviour, Strategic Leadership and Management.

Barine has authored and co-authored several books among them *Rediscovering Leadership: Principles to launch and grow your leadership*, (2006) *Successful Leadership: 8 essential principles that you must know*, (2007), *Transformational Leadership in the Local Church*, A training manual for

the Transformational Church Leadership program of PAC University, (2009), *Leading With your Heart*, (2013), *Leading with your Head* (2014), and *Leading with your Hands* (2014). He has also co-authored *Transformational Corporate Leadership* (2011), *A Life Well Lived: living to leave a Legacy*, (2009) and *The Kenya National Anthem: Our prayer & heritage* (2012) as well as contributing articles in various magazines around the world.

Barine enjoys continuous learning and hence teaches Leadership Governance & Business courses at St. Paul's University as an adjunct faculty member in the MBA & BALM programs. In addition, he has supervised students doing their Research Projects at the same University as well as Pan Africa Christian University in their Leadership program. Barine has consulted for many public and private sector organizations and enjoys training and facilitating workshops and seminars around the globe.

Prof. DAVID MINJA

Prof. David Minja is an Associate Professor of Management at Kenyatta University in the Department of Public policy and Administration. He previously held the same position at Kenya School of Government. Prior to his appointment as Associate Professor, he was Dean and Senior Lecturer, Faculty of Business and Communication at St. Paul's University. He has worked at the Ministry of Finance (Treasury), K-Rep Bank, Ewaso Nyiro South Development Authority as a Senior Economist/Head of Planning and Ag. Managing Director in the same organization. He later became the CEO of the Local Authorities Pension Trust. He holds a Doctorate in Organizational Development and Transformation from CEBU Doctor's University (Philippines), Masters in Business Administration (MBA) from Newport University, Master of Arts in Leadership from Pan Africa Christian University & Trinity Western University (Canada) and a BA in Economics and Business from Kenyatta University.

His research, teaching and consulting interests are in the areas of Organizational Development and Change, Human Resource Management, Strategic Management, Leadership and Governance. He has published many papers in refereed journals in the areas of ethics, leadership and organizational transformation. He is also the co-author of *Industrial Relations in Kenya: Principles & Practices* (2009). He has also co-authored *Transformational Corporate Leadership* (2011) and two more books in public sector leadership and managing organizational change, which are to be released soon.

Prof. Minja is also a consultant for many public and private sectors organizations. He is also a resource person for Commission of University Education in matters of accreditation of degree programs in Kenya and quality assurance in higher education.

JOHN MUHOHO KIMANI

Dr. John Muhoho is acting Academic Registrar at St. Paul's University. He has served as a Head of Department in the faculty of Business and Communication Studies. He is a faculty member and a specialist in Strategic and Financial Management and has taught as an adjunct lecturer in many universities including Kenyatta, Moi and Daystar University.

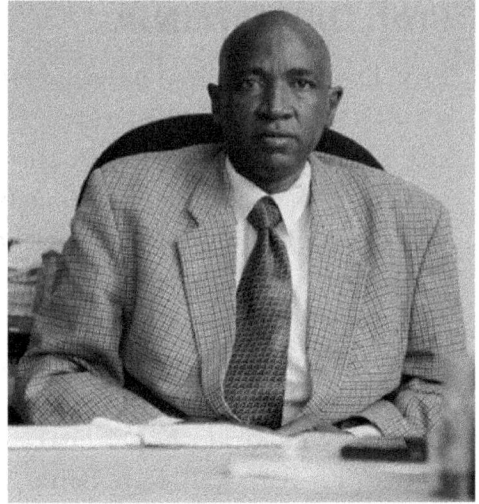

He formally worked as a 'Finance Director at the Anglican Church of Kenya and a Treasurer of Conference of All Anglican Provinces in Africa(CAPA).

He obtained his doctorate degree at CEBU University in Philippines, Master's degree in Strategic Management from the University of Nairobi and Bachelor of economics from Egerton University.

He is a Certified Public Accountant, CPA (K) and Certified Public Secretary, CPS (K). He is a member of Institute of Certified Public Accountants of Kenya (ICPAK) and a member Institute of Public Secretaries of Kenya (ICPSK). His areas of competence, research and consultancy are organizational development and transformation, strategic change management, system thinking and strategic financial management. He has supervised postgraduate students specializing in these areas. He has also written journal articles and modules in these areas.

Muhoho also served as a member of task team for Commission of University Education (CUE) that developed the credit transfer and accumulation system for the Master of Business Administration (MBA) programmes in Kenya in 2012.

www.ingramcontent.com/pod-product-compliance
Lightning Source LLC
Chambersburg PA
CBHW071555200326
41519CB00021BB/6759